Julia Pastrana

The Tragic Story of the
Victorian Ape Woman

D1331708

JULIA PASTRANA

THE TRAGIC STORY OF THE
VICTORIAN APE WOMAN

**CHRISTOPHER HALS GYLSETH
& LARS O. TOVERUD**

Translated by Donald Tumasonis

SUTTON PUBLISHING

This book was first published as *Julia Pastrana – Apekvinnen*
by Forlaget Press, 2001

First published by Sutton Publishing Limited in 2003

This paperback edition first published in 2004 by
Sutton Publishing Limited · Phoenix Mill
Thrupp · Stroud · Gloucestershire · GL5 1RW

British Library Cataloguing in Publication Data
A catalogue record for this book is available from the British
Library.

ISBN 0 7509 3313 5

Typeset in 11/14pt Photina.
Typesetting and origination by
Sutton Publishing Limited.
Printed and bound in Great Britain by
J.H. Haynes & Co. Ltd, Sparkford.

Contents

Acknowledgements

The authors particularly wish to thank the following: first and foremost, our knowledgeable and enthusiastic translator, Donald Tumasonis, who also did a lot of valuable research for this book. Next, the extremely knowledgeable collector and 'freakophile', Jan R. Bruun; publishing editor, carnival expert and proprietor of the private entertainment collection 'The Merry Archive', Herman Berthelsen; carnival director Bjørn Lund; Per Madsen, head consultant at the National Archives (*Riksarkivet*); high school teacher and author Magne Aasbrenn; Anne Karin Sønsteby at the Military Museum's library; archivists at the Oslo newspapers *Dagbladet*, *VG* and *Aftenposten*. The Lerfald family in Fredrikstad gave us access to the late Georg Lerfald's comprehensive memoirs and photographs from the carnival business. Nora Vike expertly translated source material from the German. In England we received much help from Dr Vanessa Toulmin during our visit to the National Fairground Archive, Great Britain's largest public archive of circus, carnival, and freakshow-related materials, at the University of Sheffield. In London, Tina Craig of the Royal College of Surgeons helped obtain important pictorial material. Our contacts in Scotland were technical conservator Brian MacLaughlin and Judith Bowers at Britannica Panopticon. In addition, the legendary American freakshow owner Ward Hall, with over fifty years in the business, contributed memories of Julia. And Bob Blackmar, publisher over many years of his own freakshow *Sideshow Newsletter*, also contributed with material from his archives.

A big thanks to all of the above, and to all those who have contributed along the way.

Picture Credits

The authors and publisher are grateful for permission to reproduce the illustrations:

Amusement Business, Nashville, Tenn.; Allers Familie-Journal, 1933; Bjørn Lund, Lund's Tivoli; British Library, London; Georg Lerfald (deceased); Harvard Theatre Collection, Houghton Library; Jan R. Bruun; Lindgren, *Emil in the Soup Tureen*, 1963; Miles, 'Julia Pastrana'; National Fairground Archive, Sheffield, UK; NTB (press service); Ødegaard, *Den store tiviboka*, 1986; Purcell, *Special Cases*, 1997; Rolf Olsson, Scandia Photopress, Malmø; Royal College of Surgeons of England, Buckland Collection; Scanpix; Sheridan, *Penny Theatres of Victorian London*, 1981; Sindre Hovdenakk; St Petersburg Circus Museum, Russia.

Preface

Hidden deep in the vaults of Oslo's National Hospital lie the remains of an extraordinary woman. Julia Pastrana was once a show business superstar – fêted throughout the world. P.T. Barnum, the great circus king, met and admired her, and wanted her in his show. Charles Darwin wrote that she was 'a remarkably fine woman'. She danced and sang in London's Regent Street, advertised as the 'Baboon Lady'. The French labelled her 'an insult to all propriety and dignity'. Poems and plays celebrated her unique qualities, while most people saw her as a freak of nature. She married her manager and had a baby son, but she and the infant died almost immediately. Her mummified body was exhibited around the world to make a quick profit in travelling shows. But when did her story begin?

In the vaults in Oslo, the flickering light reveals the contents of the hospital's basement room. Between the grey and windowless concrete walls, under weak lighting, time stands still. And all at once, you are inside medicine's innermost chamber of horrors. Twisted shadows are cast upon the walls, which are decked from floor to ceiling with half-empty shelves of wood and metal packed with glass bottles of different sizes, some as small as milk cartons, others a foot wide and over three feet high. Light filters through turbid liquids of varying colour and uncertain composition to reveal a macabre collection of body parts. An amputated foot, a pale hand the colour of wax, a human embryo, a greyish brain, something of knotty, indefinable form (a tumour?), a detached, deformed elbow. Numerous flasks are filled with human abnormalities, swaying ghost-like, weightlessly. They are weakly illuminated from above; many have handwritten, yellowing labels. Dust and silence everywhere. In dark corners, folders and archives are hidden behind all kinds of remarkable objects.

In one far corner, there is an indeterminate apparition. Totally covered by a black refuse sack, about five feet high, it has vaguely human contours. What is it? A stuffed ape?

1

A Sympathetic, Intelligent Monster

In western Mexico, one dark night, in the coastal province of Sinaloa, a mild, wet wind is blowing up from the sea, up towards the great forests inland. The air is heavy, and the breeze pleasant, not least to a young Indian woman who lies on a couch waiting to give birth. She is one of the so-called root-digger Indians,[1] a small group of natives of short stature with long, bristly black hair, who live by gathering and collecting roots and plants. In the Sinaloa forests, between the many rivers running from the highlands below the Sierra Madre Mountains down to the coast, the vegetation is thick and lush. And here the Indians have set up camp, in anticipation of the birth.

The heavily pregnant woman soon withdraws from the others, as is the custom,[2] and finds a suitable spot far away from the camp. There she squats, tightening a belt around her waist, supporting herself against a tree. There is nothing else to do but wait and hope. Suddenly, a horrified shriek echoes through the forest. The child has arrived. The disaster is a fact.

With her newborn child in her arms, the young woman sits on the ground, crying, despairing, alone. She knows something is terribly wrong. This child will bring much sorrow, and nothing will remain the same. 'Naualli,'[3] she murmurs with fear in her voice, while the baby girl turns its grotesque face towards her.

What happened after this, no one knows for sure. Perhaps the mother chose to go deeper into the forest, away from the tribesmen. Or perhaps she went back to camp, only to be chased away with threats and curses. But she certainly disappeared from the tribe, and her tragic fate was sealed, without anyone lifting a finger to help. She and her baby would probably die in the wilderness, among wild beasts and evil spirits – unless they had already made a pact with the devil.

But why did she murmur 'Naualli'? Mexico's Indians have had myths about *naualli*, evil supernatural beings, since the Aztec era in the sixteenth century. The Aztec word for wizard was *Nuahualli*, and the idea of the bloodthirsty Mexican werewolf grew from that. A naualli is a shapeshifter who can change into a black coyote, a prairie wolf or other dangerous animal. It then attacks humans, preferably children, and tears them to pieces in a terrible rage. It is said that naualli make deals with the devil to obtain the power of changing form, and to be able to drink human blood. Such a werewolf can also influence the life inside a womb, and is thus used to explain stillbirths and deformed babies. The devil of the Indians is a gruesome creature, always portrayed with a black beard which was particularly repulsive because facial hair was uncommon among Indians. When on rare occasions such hair does appear, it is plucked out as soon as possible. *Shabótshi* – the bearded ones – is the word used by the Sinaloa Indians for Mexicans of Spanish descent.

Two years after the birth of the child, in 1836, a group of Mexican herders in the Sinaloa highlands were looking for a missing cow. Instead, they found a young Indian woman out in the wilderness, in a hidden mountain cave. She called herself Espinosa, was shy and afraid, and carried a small child. After the woman had calmed down, she said the child wasn't really hers, while at the same time giving signs of being strongly attached to the little one. When the herders took a closer look at it, they understood why she denied being the mother. This was no ordinary child; in fact, they had never seen anything like it. They crossed themselves in fear and disbelief.

Could it really be a human child? It looked like a monkey, with thick black hair over its entire body, big lips and a protruding muzzle. The eyes and behaviour nonetheless showed that it was a human being, a healthy and alert little girl. The woman claimed that she and the baby were being held prisoners in the cave by an enemy tribe of Indians. The herders saw no sign of anyone else, and were uncertain what to believe. Nonetheless, as good Catholics, compelled to help in the name of compassion, they decided to take the pair to the nearest city. The woman with the remarkable furry child followed, obediently, on the road to civilisation.

THE ONLY ONE OF ITS KIND

Mexico was then a young country, and only fifteen years had passed since its independence from colonial Spain in 1821. After four centuries of exploitation, a modern state was being built from the ground up, and the way ahead was long. The country had been plundered of its silver, gold and other resources, and ownership of the land was shared between the Church and the nobility; poverty was great. But when, in 1824, Mexico did get a new constitution and declared itself a federal republic it was hoped that law and order would replace the lawlessness and political unrest that had prevailed previously. In the country's states, local committees were formed which, to their best ability, created a legal framework. As with several other newly founded nations, French legal principles and the French constitution were the basis of the new judicial and political system. France represented an ideal, both culturally and politically, and Mexico's elite were influenced by this just as much as anybody else.

There were enlightened people in the provinces, too, and in Sinaloa it was from them that members of the legislative assembly were drawn. In December 1831 a constitutional meeting was held in the provincial capital, Culiacán, to establish Sinaloa's sovereignty and to begin work on the state's own laws. The assembly's president was the scholarly, highly educated Pedro Sánchez whose performance drew praise, beginning a career that would take him to the summit of local society. But a strange twist of fate awaited him, although neither he nor the Indian woman, Espinosa, had a clue about that. But what had happened to her meanwhile?[4]

When the herders had reached a populated area, the hairy little girl was taken from Espinosa, who had after all denied that she was the mother. And how could she possibly have supported them both? She should have been happy for someone to look after the child, and that's what the authorities did, baptising and placing her in a children's refuge in Culiacán. They called her Julia Pastrana, an Hispano-Mexican name as good as any. Whatever Indian name she might have had was of no interest. Julia was now a registered citizen of the newly founded country of Mexico, and she soon learned to speak fluent Spanish. Nothing wrong with her mind and wit, said the staff at the refuge to the visitors who arrived to see the bearded girl.

No one there called her child of evil, even though she had hair on her body and face. No one called her naualli or devil, or chased her away. Julia was a local celebrity. When the honourable Pedro Sánchez took office on 3 June 1837 as the state of Sinaloa's tenth governor, it marked a turning point in her life. Poor, and without parents, she did not know of the powerful Señor Sánchez. He, however, was well informed about her, by reputation at least. And now, by virtue of his new position and in his enormous governor's palace, he considered a small experiment. He contacted the orphanage and said he wanted the remarkable child to be sent over as soon as possible. It would amuse him to have her in the house and she could be his maid when she grew older. Besides, in the name of humanity and science, it would be interesting to see how she took to learning. And, as it happened, with lessons in the governor's library, she did well.

Perhaps she found, in that good Catholic home, a book with the legend of St Wilgefortis, who is claimed as the only female saint with a beard. Medieval Wilgefortis was the daughter of a heathen king of Portugal, the story goes. The king wanted to marry her to another pagan monarch; Wilgefortis, strong in her faith, despaired. She prayed to God to spare her from such a horrible fate and, in answer, miraculously received her luxurious beard. Now well and truly unsuitable for the marriage market, her enraged father had her crucified.

In another version, Wilgefortis was out in the forest when a nobleman forced his attentions on her. She fled and he followed. In despair, she called on God, and the beard was sent from heaven. The nobleman was struck with fear and loathing, and Wilgefortis was briefly saved. When she returned home and told her father the story, he thought she was lying. God must have sent her the beard, he reasoned, as a punishment for her impropriety with the nobleman. And that's why she was crucified.

The stories about Wilgefortis were long thought to be true, although they were later claimed to be the result of a misunderstanding. It is thought that the robed Christ-figure of Lucca's Santo Volto[5] led the simple-minded to think it was a crucified woman. In some processions, the robe looked almost like a woman's dress, and was possibly the origin of the story of Wilgefortis, although this has lately been contested in academic circles. In any event, many European women are said to have prayed to her to help them get rid of troublesome spouses. Beards, however, they did not get, unlike the young Julia Pastrana in Mexico, who no doubt believed that she was the only one in the world to be doomed to a life of such loneliness. Could any man ever love a bearded woman? And would she ever find such a man? It seemed doubtful. And if it occurred, would he love her for her own sake? Only time would tell; and she had other things to think about.

A CURIOSITY AND A MONSTROSITY

Julia soon became part of the household, and lived a relatively good life. She had to work hard, but was able to learn. The alternatives for an orphaned and mis-shapen Indian girl were grim – poverty and dire need. Julia was lucky, and, even though Sánchez left his post as governor after one short year, she stayed with the family when they left the palace. After a while Sánchez said that he would gladly be her official guardian. And so it happened: Julia found a home and lived a respectable life, against all the odds.

She grew up to become in many ways a normal young woman, as far as circumstances allowed. She reached a height of four and a half feet, not abnormally short for Indians like herself, and developed a round and womanly figure. Her shoulders were broad and shapely, and her arms, legs, hands and feet were of proper proportions, even though her skin was covered almost entirely by thick, dark hair. Her face was broad, with quite a low hairline and a thick growth of beard by the ears, around the mouth and under the chin. Her mouth jutted forward prominently, with unusually large lips, and a broad, flat nose. Her ears were quite large, as were her eyes which had a reserved, restrained expression.

Julia knew that she was different, and was used to being stared at. She could nonetheless smile radiantly, it was said, especially when allowed to sing and dance. Or when someone took the time to speak to her, or teach her something new. She spoke Spanish and English, and a bit of French, but what little she knew of her native Indian language had long been forgotten. She had been coached in domestic and household activities, and loved to read. What she knew of the world she had learned from the library of the house. She had grown to adulthood entirely under the supervision of others.

But by April 1854, when Julia was twenty, she no longer felt welcome in the Sánchez family home. And she was tired of Culiacán, where she was viewed everywhere as ugly and different. Perhaps something had occurred between her and Sánchez? Or maybe his family wanted her out of the house, now that she was old enough to take care of herself? In any case, Julia felt herself ill-treated, and said that she wanted to return to her Indian relatives. Everyone knew this was just wishful thinking. Inwardly, Julia knew it too, but what could she do? She was alone, among people of a different culture who saw her as a curiosity and a monstrosity.

A sympathetic and intelligent monster, admittedly, but still essentially different in herself, a total outsider. No one stopped her from going, and she was soon on her way. Where to? She hardly knew. Any place away from where she had spent the last seventeen years. Perhaps she was considering some remote part of the country where she might find peace and meet others of her kind. But

she would never get that far. For her there could be no
way back.

There were, however, other directions to follow, though
they might have seemed beyond the furthest reach of her
imagination. On this first journey of hers, greater than
anything she had done previously, about to leave her old life,
Julia Pastrana met a well-dressed stranger. He introduced
himself as Mr Rates, an American impresario and
professional showman with good contacts in New York. He
was well-spoken, polite and attentive, and showed great
interest in Julia's appearance. She was very special, he said.
In New York she would be a sensation, and Rates asked her
outright if she might not consider a life on the stage.

She could already sing and dance. She could sew her own
clothing, both everyday wear and fine dresses with silk and
embroidery, so costumes would be no problem. Rates
assured her that she'd get a considerable income and be well
cared for. Julia thought it over, and decided quickly.

2

The Mysterious Animal

In December 1854 New York saw the opening of a spectacular show at the Gothic Hall musical theatre at 316 Broadway. According to advance publicity, spectators could see 'the Marvellous Hybrid or Bear Woman', a singular sensation of international calibre. No one had ever seen anything like it, the doorman insisted: 'So grab the chance! Come inside and see with your own eyes . . . The unbelievable, the fantastic, the unique . . . Hybrid of animal and human . . . The one and only Bear Woman from the wilds of Mexico!'

Huge crowds streamed in, more than anyone expected. The theatre's gaudy hall, where meals and entertainment were served simultaneously, was soon filled with a noisy, expectant audience. The air was thick with smoke and the reek of alcohol; sweat and damp rose from heavy winter coats. There was clinking of glasses, loud laughter, and the tuneless tinkling of a piano in the background when, suddenly, Rates came on to the stage and introduced the main act. Silence. The curtains slowly opened. A small form in a red dress stepped carefully into the light.

At this time New York was one of the most exciting and promising cities in America. It was also one of the most brutal and chaotic.[1] The city was small in area, with more than 600,000 inhabitants: the overcrowding was unbelievable. Regular street battles occurred between gangs of different nationalities, and thousands of street arabs begged and stole. The police and fire services were only loosely organised, and the city's politics was rotten with corruption. There were sordid dives and bordellos on every other corner, but there were also more than 250 houses of worship. To the consolation or despair of the wave of immigrants who came to the city around the middle of the century, everything was there. In 1852 alone, more than 300,000 entered New York harbour. Most remained unemployed for years. Illness and criminality set in. Life was hard in the metropolis, and the search for amusement was an important part of daily life.

At the corner of Broadway and Ann Street was the town's biggest entertainment centre, the P.T. Barnum Museum. No one had seen a more extraordinary, remarkable place, with its displays and stage shows, curiosities, carnivals, and museums. There were jugglers, sword swallowers, snake charmers, strongmen and fakirs. In addition to the authentic freakshows, the unusual, the deformed and the mentally retarded also performed on stage. There were Siamese twins and people without limbs, fat ladies and skinny men, people with crocodile skin, wildmen from Africa, dwarfs and giants.

And there were bearded ladies. With his sharp nose for business, Phineas Taylor Barnum the museum director would undoubtedly have been interested in adding Julia Pastrana to their number. But Julia was busy elsewhere. The two would come to meet a few years later, nonetheless, but it might have been better for Julia had she met him earlier.

By all accounts the famous Barnum was generous to his artists and gave them good terms. Many of his stars made large sums and then retired, but none were as wealthy as Barnum, thanks to his unique marketing skills. During his long career, he became the quintessential image of the

American showman, a self-made man with unbelievable reserves of imagination and drive. He was without doubt the nineteenth century's greatest name in entertainment, and the creator of his era's most popular show. And if P.T. Barnum had not been at this type of amusement since the 1830s, Julia Pastrana would never have gained her renown.

There had, of course, been popular entertainments with circuses, fairs, amusement parks, and museums long before Barnum's time. But the size and professionalism now changed. His secret was to give equal weight to both light entertainment and more demanding performances. His later reign as the great circus king in America and Europe was also the heyday of the sideshow. This had smallish separate tents with human freaks and other wonders as a speciality, a bit like a travelling circus. While the big top showed major acts with lion taming, elephants and high-wire acts with, in Barnum's time, up to 14,000 spectators in a single tent, midgets, giants and bearded ladies could be viewed in a corner of the grounds. And they were very good for business.

'. . . STRICTLY CHARACTERISTIC OF THE FEMALE'

Bearded ladies were not an unknown phenomenon around the middle of the nineteenth century. Any self-respecting freakshow (or that had due respect for the public's money) had one. Some were fakes with false beards and moustaches, and others were men in disguise. Others were something else again – the unique and heavily furred Mademoiselle Fanny, advertised as the 'link between humans and the beasts', was actually an ape. But there were many others who were genuine, and who let their beards grow for the sake of business.

Only a handful were like Julia Pastrana, with hair or fur over the entire body; as a rule, the bearded ladies were normal except for their facial hair. In order to present the greatest feasible contrast on stage, these women were made as feminine as possible. They had beautiful and exclusive gowns, ruched and silk ribboned, with corseted waists. Their hair was fashionably styled, and they wore large and apparent valuable jewellery. Perhaps they also sang a little melody of love, staring dreamily into space. In the exhibition brochures they were described as warm and caring, soft-spoken and faithful to their husbands – since most were married – and it was underlined how happy they were with reading and housework. They were, in short, just what a proper woman should be.

These bearded ladies often sold photographs of themselves, like almost all the freak show artists. Between shows, they sat outside their tents with large piles of pictures, cartes-de-visite, which they offered with or without signatures. Such cards were extremely popular, and often provided significant extra income. Photographs were still novelties for most people, and many collected 'freak' photographs seriously. They placed these photographs in large albums, and showed them proudly to friends and acquaintances at family parties and social occasions.

When, after 1851, it became technically possible to print large editions of photographs, freak photos became another source of income for a rapidly growing business. In Barnum's world, people who were different were big business, and the more unusual, the better. There were few, if any, restraints. For a period, so-called 'Pig-Faced Ladies' were the rage. They were exceptionally ugly short women with elongated pig-like visages. They always appeared with bonnets on their heads and mittens on their hands, for good reasons – they were really shaved bears. And the public smiled and shrugged.

One of the most successful artists, both on stage and with

pictures, was the elegant Madame Josephine Fortune Clofullia, 'the Bearded Lady of Geneva'. She was born in Switzerland in 1831, and christened Josephine Boisdechene Versoix. That was too difficult to pronounce for the average American, hence Madame Clofullia. In the 1850s she was a fêted star at Barnum's in New York. On stage she appeared almost dripping with diamonds, in a ball gown, with a tiara on her head, and took the public by storm. On a later nine-month tour, she pulled in hundreds of thousands of paying spectators to Barnum's circus shows, making all parties happy.

Clofullia was known for her beauty, but best of all for her long and full beard. She consciously trimmed it in the same style as the French Emperor Napoleon III, which rather irritated the empress. As it was, her husband was rather taken by the beautiful Clofullia, and it was he who gave her the diamonds. In fact, this was not unusual: nobility and royalty often gave gifts to 'freaks', sometimes valuable jewellery and art. Indeed, the most famous midget in the United States, 'General Tom Thumb', toured Europe with Barnum and received a miniature gilt carriole with matching ponies from Queen Victoria.

Madame Clofullia also visited England, though without an audience with the Queen. During one early appearance in London, she was examined at Charing Cross Hospital where a doctor by the name of W.D. Chowne verified that her beard was real and that 'her breasts [are] . . . large and fair, and strictly characteristic of the female'.[2] As indisputable proof of her femininity, Clofullia had a child in 1851, a little girl without any superfluous hair on her face or body. Later, however, Clofullia gave birth to a bearded son, no doubt making Barnum very happy. A few years later, the little boy appeared on stage as 'Infant Esau',[3] after the biblical Esau who had hair all over his body. In the promotional brochure, Barnum said, 'His body is thoroughly covered with hair, more particularly over the shoulders and on the back; his face is fully surrounded with whiskers, fully marked and about half an inch in length, but of light colour. The child is strong and healthy and promises fair to astonish the reader.'[4] Spectators, and perhaps the child's mother, were even more astounded when Barnum began to deck the boy out in women's clothes. This went on until he was fourteen years old. The reasoning was simple – a bearded boy is remarkable but a bearded girl is even better.

As for Clofullia, even though she had given birth, had large breasts, and was a great beauty, not everyone believed in her gender. During her very first appearance at Barnum's Museum, while stepping out on stage nervous and unwell in her new ball gown, a deep voice called out from the audience: 'This is a swindle. She's a swindler, a man in a dress! Throw him out! We want our money back!' The bearded lady from Geneva broke down in tears, suggesting her femininity, while the public became more and more agitated. In a flash, director Barnum himself stepped out on stage, and asked in a stentorian voice who dared claim that he dealt in swindles and tricks. A man in the crowd answered, and Barnum replied that he'd see him in court. Fine, came the reply, any time at all! The public hooted, and Barnum politely asked Madame Clofullia to continue the show. And the case really did go to court, with three different doctors examining the bearded lady and confirming beyond a shadow of a doubt that she was a woman. Her father and husband also appeared as witnesses, and the newspapers wallowed in good sensational muck. What almost no one knew was that the barracker in the hall had been, in all likelihood, hired and paid by Barnum. The director laughed longest and last, as usual. This was not the last time he went to court fighting claims about alleged swindling and trickery.

'A SUCKER BORN EVERY MINUTE'

P.T. Barnum was the greatest practitioner at the art of putting one over on the public, even though some thought they could beat him at his own game. As a rule, the attempts failed, as they did in the case of the Cardiff Giant.[5] That story began with the bright idea of cigar manufacturer George Hull from Binghamton, New York, in 1868. An atheist provoked by biblical discussions, he decided to carry out a large-scale hoax and profit from the widespread interest in excavations and ancient finds. He located a gypsum quarry in Iowa, and had a large block carved out, bringing it to a stonecutter in Chicago. He said he wanted the block formed into a giant human shape, to resemble both a fossilised body and a sculpture. When finished, it was over ten feet long, with full details such as arteries and fingernails, and lay with one hand on its stomach. By rail and wagon, Hull trundled the giant out to a cousin with a farm in the country town of Cardiff, New York, and buried it.

A few months later, Hull told his cousin who was in on the swindle to drill a well, right over the spot where the giant lay buried. The work started, they waited and sure enough, the excavators came running. They'd hit something big in the ground, like they'd never seen before. The giant was dug out, and the newspapers made a sensation of it. Everybody assumed that the giant was real. The masses come to the farm like pilgrims, and a tent was set up around the site: admission fifty cents.

Only a few days after the find, Hull sold the major share in it for tens of thousands of dollars. The new owners moved the statue to the nearby city of Syracuse, and built a large hall to house it. The viewing price went up to one dollar, and the money still poured in. At that point, P.T. Barnum entered the fray. He sent an agent to see the exhibition, and offered $50,000 to buy it. But the owners wouldn't sell. Barnum despaired. The giant was the country's most talked-about attraction. Then the circus king got an idea – he'd carve his own giant. He put it on view, and cheekily claimed that this was the Cardiff Giant, which he had purchased from the owner. The other was the fake! As usual, Barnum got a lot of attention. Many newspapers repeated his claim, and the owners of the original giant lost money. And while this was happening one of the owners, thinking of all those running to view Barnum's fake giant, was credited with saying, 'There's a sucker born every minute.'

The saying soon became a common catchphrase, often attributed to Barnum himself, though its true origins probably go back much further.

The owners sought an injunction against Barnum, but since Hull had already admitted the fraud in a Syracuse newspaper, the judge decided that Barnum could not be punished for having called the original giant a fake. The moral of this story is unclear. More clear is the story's immoral aspect, although no one gets particularly excited about it. The public, those 'suckers born every minute', are dished out with exactly what they want. After that, they are normally satisfied, as Barnum had always understood.

The young Barnum had first arrived in the big city early in the 1830s, with a wife and young daughter and without a dollar in his pocket. His finances changed quickly when he read in the newspaper about an old slave woman, Joice Heth, who claimed to have been George Washington's nurse. Even though the president had been dead for thirty years, and the woman proved to be only seventy-nine years old, Barnum did not let such trifles stop him. Knowing the magic effect the name Washington had on American hearts, he borrowed money and bought the woman out of slavery. Then he began a comprehensive advertising campaign to draw people to the exhibition of Washington's nurse – and not only that, she was America's oldest woman. With his giant announcements in all the newspapers, the distribution of handbills, large posters on fences and public transport, the trick worked. Joice Heth became the hottest topic in town. Barnum earned $4,000 in a year. The only problem was that 'America's oldest woman' died from all the excitement. It was a tough break for Barnum, but he didn't give up.

With money he had saved he started a travelling circus, which he sent on tour for as long as the money held out. Going bankrupt, he went back to New York. Later, he was often on the road again, at times with fabulous success, but that was far in the future. Not long after the first failure, his next project was the publication of an edifying Sunday paper, advocating Christianity and temperance. A man of inner contradictions, Barnum was both moralist and huckster. In the end, show business was more fun. Having visited the American Museum in New York, full of curiosities from around the world, he took it over and began a new advertising campaign. With that, his fortune was made.

P.T. Barnum's Museum was at the height of its fame in the late 1850s, and its freak show inspired showmen of more modest talents. Many had only one or two artists under them, as was the case with Mr Rates and Julia. From Barnum, they learned to promote loudly. No lie or exaggeration was too great, no claim too unbelievable when a show was being sold to the public. Barnum had been the first to understand the necessity of advertising on a large scale. He also understood that the public loved to be fooled, as long as they were entertained along the way. Nonetheless, he kept to the faith of his childhood, and would not serve alcohol to visitors. His museum was meant to be a family place, not a source of drunkenness and depravity. There was enough of that in town already.

'WITH A DETESTABLE SENSUALITY'

'[The] most unspeakable abomination and the basest stain
on the metropolis': that was printed in the *New York World*
in 1862 as an indignant cry for moral reform.[6] The topic
was the town's many saloons and 'houses of entertainment'
where drunkenness, criminality and prostitution were
flourishing. After witnessing years of abandon and gross
indecency, New York's good citizens had had enough. But
these moral watchdogs were powerless, since there was a
limitless demand for entertainment. Already in the 1830s
there had been a fine mix, with saloons for dancing,
drinking, and light entertainment, musical and comedy
halls, bordellos, gambling houses and ice cream booths.
Soon after came serious theatre, opera and philharmonic
orchestras with foreign stars on the programme, providing
civilised entertainment for the rich.

A few years later, Jenny Lind – the 'Swedish Nightingale'
– appeared at Castle Gardens. But it wasn't exciting enough
for the great majority. Nor was it for Jenny Lind, perhaps,
for she joined forces with Barnum after a while and toured
the country with him. It was light entertainment that was
popular with the greatest public, both high and low socially.
Whether they were rich or poor, audiences were fascinated
by comical, erotic and burlesque stage shows. Because of
this, New York's entertainments became a democratic arena
– dominated, it should be noted, by the male population.
The main roles for women were those of waitresses,
performers or prostitutes. Regardless of class or gender, all
were looking for money or entertainment, and Broadway
offered the most remarkable mix.

It was also the place to see the bear-woman. Rumours
about her spread rapidly across the city. Not only was she
fascinatingly ugly, but she performed Spanish dances in the

style of the well-known, glamorous dancer Lola Montez, author of *The Arts of Beauty*. The contrast was stark, and almost a parody, even though the performances were carried out with the utmost seriousness. The public was totally won over by the woman who sang Spanish folk tunes while dancing the Highland Fling.

One day Dr Alexander B. Mott, a distinguished gentleman, contacted her manager Mr Rates. He very much wanted to examine the hairy creature everyone was talking about. Purely out of scientific interest, of course. Rates nodded and smiled, and said he'd gladly be of help. Anything for science. However, private viewings in the back room were not free. Dr Mott understood perfectly, and paid without complaining.

He had inherited his taste for the unusual and bizarre from his father, the renowned surgeon and professor, Valentine Mott, famous for having carried out more than 1,000 amputations in his glory days. Furthermore, Mott the younger would go on to inherit a comprehensive collection of human medical curiosities which his father had taken a lifetime to accumulate. The jewel of the collection was a prepared human head, safely kept in the Motts' large family library. It was a mortal remnant of the proud Seminole Indian chief Osceola[6] who, after an heroic struggle, had been seized under a flag of truce by the whites. After a few pitiful months in custody, Osceola became seriously ill in 1838. He requested his trusted white doctor to ensure he was buried on his tribe's homeland in Florida. The promise was made, and Osceola died, but he was buried in an entirely different part of the country after the doctor had stolen his jewellery for souvenirs. Moreover, in all secrecy, his head was removed, since the doctor wanted it preserved for science. Later on, Mott obtained the chieftain's head, and it was proudly added to the collection.[7]

Alexander B. Mott was therefore not totally unfamiliar

with Indians when he met Julia Pastrana one December day in 1854. He was not at all certain if it was a human he saw, even though the creature shook his hand, curtsied and spoke politely to him in English. After a probing medical examination, he decided that Julia was in fact a hybrid, a mixture of human and orang-utan. He called her 'the mysterious animal', and even stated that she should really have had a tail. The lack of a tail was explained by Julia's human component which had caused it to disappear. He seemed to think this was something she should actually be happy about. After the examination, Dr Mott went happily home to tell his old father about the orang-utan hybrid, a specimen the collection lacked. Would they be able to acquire it? No one knew what Julia felt about the visit; no one cared. Certainly not Mr Rates who had just received a gilt-edged offer from another colleague. Julia changed owners without further formality. Soon she was with a new impresario, J.W. Beach.

All novelties, even the greatest, have a limited life, not least in show business where new talent is queueing up behind, and especially in fast-moving New York. Julia was one of the biggest celebrities, but Mr Beach was a careful man. Something as rare as a human-ape hybrid had to be exhibited judiciously so that the public did not tire of it. Six months in New York was enough. But then where?

To Cleveland, which had recently received a rail connection to New York. One summer day in 1855 Julia was sitting in a new railway carriage, looking at the landscape flying by. Julia's only previous journey had been from Mexico to New York, via New Orleans, so she did not complain. She wanted to be out in the world, experiencing new things, and in Cleveland she noticed the large bridge stretching over the Cuyahoga River, and discovered that the city consists of two separate parts, on opposite sides of the river. Originally two rival towns that had fought for many years for control of the river trade, in 1854, the year before Julia made her visit, they became amalgamated into one. The economy was booming, the pleasure industry was flourishing. And Julia was a sensation.

Cleveland, too, had its curious scientists, and, in August, she had to be examined again. This time, Professor S. Brainerd it was who weighed and measured, and tugged at her beard and looked down into her mouth. He plucked out a hair here and there to examine under the microscope, and at last declared that she had 'no trace of Negro blood'.[8]

He confirmed furthermore that Julia was a hybrid, as Rates had claimed, being a member of a separate species, part orang-utan and part human, and confirmed it with a certificate. Impresario Beach bowed and thanked him, and put his hybrid on display as soon as he could. According to the new exhibition folder that he had prepared, all Julia's fellow tribesmen shared her furriness. He added that all rootdigger Indians had facial features with 'a close resemblance to those of a bear or Orang Outang', and that these primitive people also had intimate relations with a number of tamed animals, including bears and apes, which could hardly be differentiated from their owners. The public was horrified and fascinated.

The orang-utan, the large primate first encountered by Europeans colonising Indonesia, was the largest and most frightening ape that most Americans were then aware of.[9] The African gorilla had only just been discovered around 1850, and news of it had not yet reached the average inhabitant of the Western world. However, its smaller relative, the orang-utan, was well-known, mainly as a symbol of everything primitive, dangerous and sexually threatening in the animal world.

Orang-utan meant 'man of the forest', Europeans were

told by the inhabitants of Sumatra and Borneo. Odoardo Beccari, an Italian explorer and naturalist who travelled in Borneo in the 1800s, wrote about the natives' experience of the orang-utan: 'The Dyaks [natives] tell many a tale about women being carried off by orangutans. No doubt the thing in itself is possible, an adult *Mayas* (orangutan) is for certain strong enough to carry off a woman.' Beccari did not believe this himself, but his readers were quite willing to give credence to the tales he told.

About two hundred years earlier, the Dutch doctor Jacob Bontius wrote regarding the origins of the orang-utan, that '[these animals] are born from the lust of Indian women, who mix with apes and monkeys with detestable sensuality'. Bontius did not believe such reports, but the myth of the orang-utan's wildness and lust became fully established. This was evident in Paris in 1825, when the dancer and actor Mazurier had a great success with the ballet *Jocko*, in which he dressed as an ape in a real ape-skin costume. Since Mazurier was an accomplished mime artist and had spent a long time studying apes' habits, the result was sensational. The audience did not know whether they were seeing a man or an ape on the stage. The mixture of fright and fascination made *Jocko* the most talked-about act of its time. It was performed across Europe and in Belgium, France, Germany and Italy and in the USA. Apes were a hot topic and the message was clear – apes like orang-utans were bloodthirsty beasts.

In 1841, Edgar Allan Poe, the American author of horror and the grotesque, published his story *The Murders in the Rue Morgue*, in which a seaman transports a giant orang-utan to Paris. The ape is kept in a cabinet in the sailor's hotel room where it observes its owner shaving. Later on, when the sailor is absent, it breaks out of its cage, grabs the razor, and tries to imitate what the sailor was doing. On his return, the seaman discovers the beast and attacks it with a whip. The orang-utan flees with the razor blade in its paw, and ends up attacking and killing local women. The story both titillated and frightened readers, reinforcing the idea that apes are terrifying creatures.

Already in 1837, the London Zoo had obtained its first baby orang-utan, Jane, who soon became a great favourite. That was a civilised exception. In Julia Pastrana's case, the comparison with apes was anything but flattering. But who cared about the truth, as long as there was a human orang-utan up on stage?

The show moved on, this time to Boston, where Julia visited the town's natural history society. Here too the enthusiastic and learned examined and peered at Julia from top to toe. The anatomist Samuel Kneeland Jr was the most thorough, and he finally rejected all earlier speculation about her beastly origin. Julia was human, and nothing else. But did anyone ask her? No. Still, she enjoyed meeting someone who treated her like an intelligent being and not like a monkey.

Of course, Julia knew that exaggeration and speculation were important aspects of publicity, but for a young woman it was highly unpleasant being known solely for her ugliness. A happier occasion occurred on the same trip, when Julia and Mr Beach went to Baltimore. They were invited to a large military ball, and Julia was the evening's highlight. With her heart in her mouth, she entered the fine ballroom, which glowed in the light from hundreds of candles in the chandeliers. It is unlikely she had ever been in a more brilliant place. Officers in uniform and ladies in gowns all came over, wanting to shake her hand. They spoke softly in a civilised fashion, and Julia answered as well as she could, smiling at everyone. Some of the gentlemen bowed, some even formally and asked if she would dance.

She was glad to. Fame had its better side, even for someone like Julia. But she was soon brought back down to earth, for in December 1855 Julia returned to New York again.

In the new year the show went to Canada. After a long tour though, demand lessened, and Beach knew that he had milked the North American market to its limits. When he received an offer from a colleague, New York impresario Theodore Lent,[10] he grabbed the opportunity. Julia was traded off, and met her fate. America, the New World, had been conquered. Europe stood waiting.

3

An Offence against all Propriety

Victorian London – centre of the world, heart of the greatest colonial empire. The largest and richest city in the West, despite a short slump in 1857, where magnificent pomp and luxury rubbed up against the most extreme poverty. This was the Dickensian cityscape of small, half-lit cobblestone streets, of smoke and fog swirling under gaslight. The American author Henry James described it thus: 'A sudden horror of the whole place came over me. . . . London was hideous, vicious, cruel, and above all overwhelming . . . she was as indifferent as was Nature herself to the single life . . . a dreadful, delightful city.'[1] Dr John Simon summed it up in an official health report about London: 'this pestilential heaping of human beings'.[2]

Pestilent or not, the town still had its colourful aspects. There was a teeming nightlife, from bordellos, sweaty boxing clubs and cheap gin mills to theatres and music halls, of which there were about forty. The music halls were especially popular; the largest accommodated over 2,000 spectators from all levels of society. Under the lights of the erotic and burlesque shows, the hotblooded men out on the town all looked alike, as they did in New York. There may have been fewer thrill-seeking rich aristocrats in Britain's more class-defined society, but the biggest attractions drew in every level of punter.

And when, in July, the newspapers announced a new attraction – 'Miss Julia Pastrana, the Nondescript, from the United States and Canada'[3] – everyone wanted a look.

'Nondescript', a word designed to titillate, was used for strange life forms, remarkable hybrids and animals not yet described by science. The advertisement also proclaimed that this singular woman had visited all large American cities, and that 'she had created the greatest possible excitement, and that the leading researchers and doctors have declared her to be one of the wonders of the world'.[4] Strictly speaking, she was not totally unknown to science but who cared about that? At the Regent Gallery in Regent Street, 'the Baboon Lady', as impresario Lent called her in the extensive brochure, was on view three times a day. Lent's twelve-page booklet described Julia's primitive origins, and her parents' close contact with bears and monkeys in the wilderness. Nonetheless this new description did tone down the animal aspect, and stressed that although Julia was a hybrid, her female human qualities prevailed over those of the orang-utan. After all, it said, she could speak three languages, and spent her childhood in a governor's home, and learned many domestic skills there. She had not yet understood the value of thinking along economic lines but 'there are hopes that she will acquire in time the money-getting faculty, equal to that of the rest of the family of man'.[5]

Yet again, Julia was a big success – many Londoners went to see her both on the stage and face-to-face after the show. As Lent wrote, 'Miss Julia is pleased when the Ladies and Gentlemen ask her questions, and examine her pretty Whiskers, of which she is very proud.'[6] How proud Julia really was of the beard it is hard to say, but she liked speaking with the public even if it only fulfilled a pent-up need for contact. Standing up there on stage could be wearisome, and she often chose to look out over the heads of the audience at the empty air. She had seen more than enough of people's expressions of revulsion and disbelief. It was different in more sociable circumstances when, for a short while at least, Julia could become a different person. In fact, ever since Lent had stopped her from wandering freely in town – for who would pay to see a bearded lady who could be seen for nothing on the street? – Julia had been very lonely. She could understand Lent's reasoning, but it was, nonetheless, a sad life she led. On the rare occasions when she went out in public she had no choice but to cover herself up, in case she frightened someone – though it was difficult for Julia to understand how that might be.[7]

In the eyes of a grim baboon!

One summer afternoon in 1857, a young civil servant was walking down Regent Street on his way home from work and came across a poster in front of an exhibition hall announcing that 'Julia Pastrana, the Nondescript, the Baboon Lady' could be seen cheaply there. Almost against his will, he was drawn inside, and what he saw affected him permanently. After the show, he staggered out, seriously shaken, physically and mentally. A creature like that he could never have imagined, even in his worst nightmare. He was a delicate man and a sensitive amateur poet. His name was Arthur Munby.[8]

Many decades later, his last collection of poems was published. The very first one is a long thirty-two stanza work entitled 'Pastrana', where the troubled impressions from his youth are presented. They begin disturbingly:

> 'Twas a big black ape from over the sea,
> And she sat on a branch of a walnut tree,
> And grinn'd and sputter'd and gazed at me
>   As I stood on the grass below:

She sputter'd and grinn'd in a fearsome way,
And put out her tongue, which was long and grey,
And hiss'd and curl'd and seem'd to say,
        'Why do you stare at me so?'

Who could help staring? I, at least,
Had never set eyes on so strange a beast –
Such a monstrous birth of the teeming East,
        Such an awkward ugly breed:
She had large red ears and a bright blue snout,
And her hairy limbs were firm and stout:
Yet still as I look'd I began to doubt
        If she were an ape indeed.

The repulsive ape-like creature is next seen in a tree in a
garden outside a German hotel where the author is staying.

But the ape still sat on that walnut bough;
And she swung to and fro, I scarce knew how,
First up in the tree, and then down below,
        In a languid leisurely dance;
And she pluck'd the green fruit with her finger'd paws
And crush'd it whole in her savage jaws,
And look'd at me, as if for applause,
        With a keen enquiring glance;

And she turn'd her head from side to side
With a satisfied air and a flutter of pride,
And gazed at herself, and fondly eyed
        Her steel-bright collar and chain:
She seem'd as blithe as a bride full-drest,
While the strong cold steel, in its slight unrest,
Did jingle and gleam on her broad black breast
        And under her shaggy mane.

But the ape-like creature gnaws wildly at her chain, and
Munby is filled with fright that she might break free.

> Perhaps she would get at me, after all!
> If the links should break, I might well feel small,
> Young as I was, and strong and tall,
>   And blest with a human shape,
> To see myself foil'd in that lonely place
> By a desperate brute with a monstrous face,
> And hugg'd to death in the foul embrace
>   Of a loathly angry ape.

The author goes up to his room to write, and goes down
again later in the day to the dining-room for dinner.
Suddenly he notices a remarkable woman at another table.
Why does she seem familiar?

> Ah, by the powers, a singular sight!
> What is that lady opposite,
> Sitting alone, with her back to the light,
>   Who has such wonderful hair?
> She is comely and young? I do not know,
> For her face shows dark in the evening glow;
> But I wonder why she looks at me so,
>   And with such an elfish stare!

Quite right, this is none other than the fearsome creature
passing itself off as a human.

> And what is that white metallic thing
> That shines on her throat, like the gleam of a ring
> Now sparkling out, now vanishing
>   As her shaggy tresses move?

I have had but a pint of Heidensack –
Yet I think of the collar and chain that deck
The broad black bosom and hairy neck
    Of that monster in the grove!

Following this, the ape-woman is overwhelmed and captured by the hotel staff and dragged back, howling and growling, into captivity. Munby lets out a sigh of relief.

As they carried her off, a cold damp sweat
Seized me all over; and yet, and yet,
I order'd my coffee and cigarette
    As usual, in the hall;
And I did not even ask of Fritz
Whether the lady were subject to fits,
Or had gone quite mad and out of her wits:
    I ask'd him nothing at all.

The poet is badly shaken by this experience, and the author considers himself lucky to have survived.

When asked how he could have chosen such an absurd theme, the peaceable Munby answered that his meeting with Julia Pastrana had made an indelible impression on him. But such a reaction was a sensitive exception. Only a tiny minority were really frightened by Julia; many people wanted to meet her in person, and certainly those who sensed her true worth.

Now and then Lent arranged exclusive showings for those especially interested so that they could experience 'The Nondescript' alone. That's how Julia met the great P.T. Barnum. One day the circus king and an English colleague paid a visit to Lent's hotel room. Barnum and Lent knew each other from New York, and both knew Julia's rarity value. When Barnum and his friend arrived they were met by a small well-dressed woman wearing a heavy veil. In a low voice she welcomed them and asked them to be seated. Then Lent came into the room. After greeting the guests, he gave Julia a discreet sign, and she removed the veil, offering herself to their gaze. The great Barnum, now famous as the world's richest and most renowned showman, was fascinated. But he wasn't able to hire her, even though that was surely what he wanted. Indeed, thirteen years later in Barnum's greatest tour ever he would proclaim among his attractions 'Giants, Dwarfs, Fijian Cannibals . . . and Digger Indians'. Julia was not the only one of her kind in show business. But she was the most hirsute, and the most famous, so Barnum was extremely interested in her. But there was nothing doing. Lent was friendly but firm: Look, but don't buy!

English doctors were not very different from their American colleagues, though perhaps not so fanciful, and many wanted to examine the ape-woman from Mexico. One of them, Dr J.Z. Laurence, wrote an article about Julia in the 11 July 1857 issue of the *Lancet*, 'A Short Account of the Bearded and Hairy Female', in which he described her precisely. Laurence wrote that she was 4ft 4in tall, with dark, thick hair over her entire body apart from her palms and the soles of her feet. Her body was powerful and well-proportioned and (he added) her breasts were surprisingly well-developed and she menstruated regularly. She was also 'intelligent and quick'. So spoke the voice of science.

That several researchers who examined hirsute women took an interest in breasts and menstruation could be seen as prurient curiosity. But there was more to it than this. There were many competing scientific theories about women, gender and hair. All the contemporary information on hairy women was summed up in the 1896 book *Anomalies and Curiosities of Medicine*. The mysteries of hair growth stood revealed:

Bearded women are not at all infrequent. Hippocrates mentions a female who grew a beard shortly after menstruation had ceased. It is a well-recognised fact that after the menopause women become more hirsute, the same being the case after the removal of any of the functional generative apparatus. Vicat saw a virgin who had a beard and Joch speaks of 'feminis barbati'. LeBlond says that certain women of Ethiopia and South America have beards and little or no menstruation. He also says that sterility and excessive chastity are causes of female beards, and cites the case . . . of a young widow who secluded herself in a cloister, and soon had a beard. Harris reports several cases of bearded women, inmates of the Coton Hill Lunatic Asylum. One of the patients was eighty-three years of age and had been insane forty-four years following a puerperal period. She would not allow the hair on her face to be cut. . . . This patient was quite womanly. The second case was a woman of thirty-six, insane from emotional melancholia. . . . The third case was that of a woman of sixty-four, who exhibited a strong passion for the male sex. Her menstruation had been regular until the menopause. She plaited her beard . . . This woman had extremely hairy legs.[9]

Research, however, marched on. In 1909 one could read the following about Julia Pastrana's condition, 'congenital hypertrichosis' (i.e. inherited excessive hirsuteness), in a Danish medical text on skin disease:

By hypertrichosis is meant an abnormal development of hair in places and at times, where it does not normally grow. Hypertrichosis can be total or local, there at birth or developed later. Total hypertrichosis is a very rare condition, which sometimes occurs over several generations of the same family. Hair growth can invade the entire body except for the palms and soles; from this derive the so-called lion-men, dog-boys, and human bears, who are of more anthropological than medical interest.[10]

That lack of medical interest derived, in all likelihood, from the condition being inherited and incurable, impervious to any ministrations. But people sharing Julia's fate weren't ignored by science because, as the book discreetly reminds us: 'The form of hypertrichosis with most interest for the doctor is that of abnormal development of facial hair in women. . . . This . . . is often the cause of a high degree of psychic depression.'[11]

When it came down to the more genetic reasons for developing hypertricosis, many years went by before science had the tools to investigate it properly.

Nobody at that time really understood that it had to do with the human skin cells and their inner relationship. There are two kinds of cells here, the so-called *epidermis*, which forms the outer layer of skin, and the *dermis*, forming the thicker skin layer underneath. Between these two layers of cells there is a molecular process going on, concerning the forming of hair follicles. A normal human body has about five million of these follicles, and the spreading of them is controlled by the relationship between the epidermis and the dermis. If the dermis sends out a signal to form more follicles than normal, the epidermis should respond negatively, so that the nearby cells do not form into follicles. In this way hair spreads on the human body in the normal way, as the individual grows up. But if, on the other hand, the molecular signals are mixed up, due to congenital hypertricosis, the dermis will keep on forming a great number of new follicles until in some cases the entire body is covered in hair. Such were the inner reasons for Julia's condition, without her ever knowing.[12]

Another visitor to Julia was the zoologist Francis Buckland,[13] who went to her London hotel room after seeing her perform at the Regent Gallery on 10 July 1857. Buckland was an expert on fish but was also interested in the bizarre. Indeed, the eleventh edition of the *Encyclopaedia Britannica* commented that his interest in anatomy led him 'to a good deal of out-of-the-way research' in zoology. It is precisely this sort of unusual research that took him to meet Julia Pastrana. The very day after they met, he sat down to write an article about her, saying amongst other things that 'her eyes were deep black and somewhat prominent, and their lids had long, thick eyelashes; her features were simply hideous'.[14] He added, though, that 'her figure was exceedingly good and graceful, and her tiny foot and well-turned ankle, *bien chausse* perfection itself'. Furthermore, he went on to say: 'She had a sweet voice, great taste in music and dancing, and could speak three languages. She was very charitable, and gave largely to local institutions from her earnings. I believe that her true history was that she was simply a deformed Mexican Indian woman.'

Even Charles Darwin got wind of Julia through his friend, the naturalist Alfred Russel Wallace. Neither had met her, but Wallace knew a dentist called Purland who at least had access to her teeth because Julia was not only abnormally hirsute but also had a rare dental condition that contributed to her remarkable appearance. In *The Variation of Animals and Plants under Domestication*, Darwin refers to his knowledge of this: 'she had a pronouncedly masculine beard and a hairy brow . . . but what concerns us, is that she in both upper and lower jaws had an irregular double set of teeth, one row placed back of the other, that Dr Purland took a cast of.

Because of this surplus of teeth, her mouth was prognathous, and the face had a gorilla-like appearance.'[15] Darwin then went on to compare Julia directly with hairless dogs (plants and animals were the book's main theme). He postulated that in the animal world skin disease could be connected with a surplus of teeth. Up to now, Julia had been compared to many types of animal, but hairless canines were a new and original twist. However, she herself would never have read this; the book came out after her death and, in all fairness, Darwin also stated that 'Miss Julia Pastrana, a Spanish dancer, was a remarkably fine woman'.

Charles Darwin may have been correct about Julia's character but scientifically he was wrong because, if anyone had bothered to ask her, she could have immediately responded that she certainly did not have any extra rows of teeth in her mouth (though she did have gum problems). Fantasising dentists must take the blame for this misunderstanding, which didn't exactly make her any less exotic in the eyes of the public. Nor was it any better when her tongue was described as large and malformed. Real people don't have four rows of teeth, deformed tongues and hair all over their bodies, do they? There could be no doubt she must be a monster, a man-beast that even science couldn't classify.

A century later an English dentist examined the same casts described by Darwin:

In the Odontological Museum is a pair of casts of the jaws of Julia Pastrana . . . which show a few unusually large teeth projecting from greatly thickened and irregular alveolar processes. It is impossible to be certain whether some prominences are projecting tooth cusps or nodules of gingiva . . . she did not possess an excessive number of teeth in double rows. . . . It appears that the

overgrowth of her gum and alveolar process was
responsible for her prognathism and what is described as
simian appearance.[16]

The gums had misled everyone because the way in which
they projected around the teeth was reminiscent of
dentition. Darwin was also wrong in stating that Dr Purland
made the casts: it was actually a dentist by the name of
Weiss. Not that it matters, but it says something about the
scientific methodology of the period.

Julia herself was not used to anything better; of all the
researchers she met and was examined by, few asked for her
own views. Any questions were directed to Theodore Lent,
and he always had an answer ready. Even respected
researchers were receptive to the most unlikely explanations,
and restraint was not always their strong suit. For Julia,
even after those uncomfortable casts had been made by the
dentist, nothing happened except for more misconceptions.
Science treated her as a 'freak' and ignored her opinions.
But what could a mis-shapen person do? There was always
someone else worse off.

. . . THE VERY INCARNATION OF LONELINESS

Victorian London had a rich diet of entertainment, of
varying tastefulness. Bearded ladies were popular, with and
without double sets of teeth, but they were not the most
incredible sight the city had to offer, nor the most disturbing.
In hidden away places in the city's back streets, the seriously
sick and deformed were put on display for little more than
small change. They were the lowest members of a freak show,
without self-respect or merit. While the elegant Madame
Clofullia, dripping with diamonds, and the celebrity dwarf
Tom Thumb were up in the first division of freak shows, with

Julia Pastrana as a less starchy alternative, there was also a mass of performers which you'd need a stronger stomach to see. All earned their daily bread on account of their physical defects and abnormalities, and almost all, even among the lowest of the low, were there of their own free will. The alternative was begging in the gutter, and almost anything was better than that.

Even so, things were so bad sometimes that the authorities intervened, not necessarily for the sake of the exploited. Some years after Julia's visit, above a derelict greengrocer's in Mile End Road, across the street from the London Hospital, London saw one of the most grotesque examples of the freak show culture. A giant banner hung over the entire shop front showing a hideous creature – a monster with human and animal traits – painted in full colour.

One witness of the remarkable show described what he had seen:

> This very crude production depicted a frightful creature that could only have been possible in a nightmare. . . . There was still more of the man than of the beast. This fact – that it was still human – was the most repellent attribute of the creature. There was nothing about it of the pitiableness of the misshapened or the deformed, nothing of the grotesqueness of the freak, but merely the loathsome insinuation of a man being changed into an animal.[17]

The writer, a doctor from a nearby hospital, intrigued by the garish banner, had ordered a private view from the show's manager, a showman of dubious character. One cold and wet November day, he gained entrance to the shop for one shilling. The place was empty, grey and sad with dust. On the shelves were abandoned, hermetically sealed tins and a few shrivelled potatoes. The lighting was dim, and the

room at first seemed empty. Right at the back was a curtain,
made of an old red tablecloth, fastened by rings to a
stretched-out cord:

> The showman pulled back the curtain and revealed a
> bent figure crouching on a stool and covered by a brown
> blanket. In front of it . . . was a large brick heated by a
> Bunsen burner. Over this the creature was huddled to
> warm itself. It never moved when the curtain was drawn
> back. Locked up in an empty shop and lit by the faint blue
> light of the gas jet, the hunched-up figure was the
> embodiment of loneliness. . . . The showman – speaking
> as if to a dog – called out harshly: 'Stand up!' The thing
> arose slowly and let the blanket that covered its head fall
> back to the floor. There stood the most disgusting
> specimen of humanity that I have ever seen.[18]

The doctor's name was Frederick Treves. He was a respected
professional, friendly and caring to his patients. Later he
was knighted and became the royal surgeon. When he met
the 'monster' in the greengrocer's he was a young, curious
doctor who had seen many strange things, including
deformities, hideous illnesses and terrible wounds. Nothing,
however, prepared him for this. He almost recoiled in horror,
even though the being was in no way wild or frightening.
Later he wrote:

> This . . . was a little man below the average height and
> made to look shorter by the bowing of his back. The most
> striking feature about him was his enormous and
> misshapened head. From the brow there projected a huge
> bony mass like a loaf, while from the back of the head
> hung a bag of spongy, fungous-looking skin, the surface
> of which was comparable to a brown cauliflower. On the

top of the skull were a few long lank hairs. The osseous growth on the forehead almost occluded one eye. The circumference of the head was no less than that of the man's waist. From the upper jaw there projected another mass of bone. It protruded from the mouth like a pink stump, turning the upper lip inside out and making of the mouth a mere slobbering aperture. . . . The nose was merely a lump of flesh. . . . The face was no more capable of expression than a block of gnarled wood.[19]

Treves was stunned as he stood and looked at the half-naked being. All visible parts of the body, with the exception of the left arm, were grotesquely deformed. Great, baggy folds of flesh hung from the back and chest, and covered the right arm. A nauseating stink hit Treves. The right hand was like a large irregular fin or paddle, with fingers like thick roots. The back was crooked because of a large hump, and the hip was obviously broken, so that the man, who was young, could only walk slowly and with great difficulty, using a cane. The face was like an ugly carnival mask. In contrast, the left arm and hand were shapely and nimble like a woman's, with small, elegant fingers and perfect skin, almost a parody of the body's hideousness. The young man's name was Joseph Merrick – and he was known as the Elephant Man.[20]

Like many of his colleagues, Frederick Treves was an inquisitive soul, with an interest in all aspects of humanity. He arranged for Merrick to visit the hospital for a closer examination and, to make it easier for the young man to get in, gave him a calling card. That card changed the Elephant Man's life. He turned up at the hospital a few days later to be used in a lecture for the Pathological Society of London. Treves got no deeper impression of Merrick's personality because the man's shyness and speech impediments made communication difficult. He assumed that Merrick was mentally deficient and left it at that. After the lecture, the Elephant Man was sent on his way. As far as Treves was concerned, the matter was closed. Later, he saw that the show had been closed by the police, and that the shop now stood empty.

Merrick and the showman were meanwhile travelling from town to town, as the police kept moving them on because such exhibitions were morally corrupt. But it was not Merrick's moral welfare that was of concern. After all, he was only a disgusting stinking monster. It was the public who needed protection, for the sake of propriety. There was a need to maintain public calm and order. Certainly, it must be dangerous for weak and pregnant women to view such things. Who knew what effect the sight of such a mis-shapen monster might have on the development of a child in the womb? In the end, the desperate showman left England for France. For a long while, they tried their luck on the continent, but things didn't go well there, either. They ended up in Brussels, and the police visited them once again. The exhibition was thought brutal, improper and immoral, and the Belgian authorities wanted them out of the country immediately.

That was it for the manager. The Elephant Man was no longer a financial asset but an economic liability. He had to be fed even when he wasn't bringing in the money. Merrick was given a ticket back to England and told to look after himself. His savings were kept by the manager to cover expenses. Without family, without a single friend, and with no other course of action open to him, Merrick returned to London and found himself on the streets.

Once there he was harassed and pestered by street urchins and riffraff until the police arrived and took him away. He could not make himself understood, and the police had no idea what to do. Finally, they searched his clothes and found nothing but a wrinkled calling card in the name of Frederick Treves, London Hospital. The police contacted the hospital, and Treves sent word that he would take in the exhausted man. Merrick arrived at the hospital, was washed and cleaned, and given clean clothing and warm food. The hospital discovered that he was not retarded but, on the contrary, sensitive and intelligent. He loved to read romantic books and, after a while, began to have long, intimate conversations with Treves. It was quite possible to understand him, but it took time and patience. No one had bothered before. His life was now totally changed, and he soon got his own room in the back of the hospital. He could stay as long as he wanted.

Every day, Treves was amazed by his new friend, his good humour and bright view of the world. Merrick never said an unkind word about anyone, and was eternally grateful for the least sign of friendliness. To the surprise of Treves, Merrick said the freak show idea had been his own, and that he himself went to the manager and proposed that he should be exhibited for money. He had spent several years in a public asylum, and couldn't take it any more. The side-show life, regardless of its horrors, had also been his salvation, no matter how strange that might seem.

Joseph Merrick was soon presented to Treves's cultured friends in London society. They treated the Elephant Man with friendliness. He was an immediate success, and quickly gained admirers among the nobility, and even in royal circles. Fame followed. Beautiful women came to visit. His room filled up with expensive presents. In his new clothes he could believe that he passed for normal. Treves discreetly hindered his access to mirrors. 'I am happy every hour of the day,' Merrick said.[21] But one night his enormous head slid from the pillow, blocking his air passages. The next day a nurse found him dead after four years in the hospital. But he did die happy and well cared for.

The story of Merrick's life is an example of the most extreme human degradation, simultaneously awful and gripping. Nonetheless, there is only one thing of real significance about him, for both his time and ours, his appearance.

His appearance brought him misfortune and pain in his childhood, put him in an asylum in his teens, and later gave him his identity as a freak – as the Elephant Man. It was his appearance and its effect upon the public that made police close the shows down, not any human respect for Merrick. And it was his deformity that put him in touch with his saviour Frederick Treves and the upper echelons of London society. His horrific appearance was his claim to fame. And this fame, a century later, produced a play and a film devoted exclusively to his story, and several books. But even then, it was his appearance – his hump, his wrinkled skin, his enormous head – that defined him. It could not be otherwise, for this is the essence of the freak show. But for nineteenth-century freaks, be they dwarf, elephant man or bearded lady, this is of no consequence. It is their life, their occupation. From the stage, any public is good public, whether repelled or uplifted. The audience's feelings mean nothing, so long as they pay. Even an ape-woman must earn a living.

. . . LONG LOCKS GROWING ON THE MIDDLE OF THE NOSE

In November 1857, the Kroll Theatre in Leipzig announced the opening of *Der Curierte Meyer* (*The Milkman Cured*), and that the public would have seen nothing like it before. One of the leading roles was to be played by a foreign star, for whom the piece had been written. She had come to Germany all the way from the United States and England, the posters read. The public could not wait, and after the excited anticipation before the curtain rose, laughter soon broke out and the audience was engrossed. The play concerns a milkman who falls in love with a young woman, whose face is always veiled. She keeps her suitor at arm's length, to his great despair. Each time he leaves the stage, she turns to the audience and does her special routine: she lifts her veil for a few short seconds. With laughter reaching new heights, the milkman returns, she drops the veil and the farce continues. This is repeated with different variations over several acts until the woman finally shows her face to the love-smitten man. He is stricken with horror, and the audience hoots again. The curtain comes down and Julia Pastrana takes the applause, centre stage.

The next day, she is back on stage but this time, when the curtain falls, that is the end. The police arrive and close down the play. It is morally abhorrent. Lent is enraged, and Julia in despair, but they can do nothing. It becomes worse when a pediatrician turns up and warns against Julia's shock effect upon the pregnant when she suddenly shows her ugly face. Good Germans cannot condone this. The travesty must go. *The Milkman Cured* closes, and Julia is unemployed.

Still, Lent didn't give up. He negotiated with the authorities and eventually got permission to exhibit Julia in what were considered more decent ways. She was allowed to perform her Spanish dances and sing folksong melodies – these would not disturb the public's peace of mind. But be warned, said the authorities, anything comic, anything improper, just once – and they would be thrown out of town. There was no chance of that. Lent and Julia had learned their lesson. Even before Leipzig they had experienced similar problems in Berlin when they arrived from London.

In Berlin, the authorities had been sceptical about such freak shows, but they reluctantly sanctioned the song and dance act after Lent had guaranteed that nothing untoward or offensive would take place on stage. The Leipzig episode left them tired and disappointed by German officials, but they received much publicity when the show closed. A journalist from the weekly *Gartenlaube* asked if he could write about Julia while she was drawn by the artist Herbert König. Lent beamed at this idea – good publicity, and, even better, it was free. It was money that mattered, and that was the impression that the journalist received while he interviewed the remarkable bearded lady. She was sweet and pleasant, and spoke openly about her many travels and appearances around the world. She also mentioned the more than twenty offers of marriage she had received along the way, and which she had rejected without hesitation. None of the men had enough money, she explained with a shy smile. Later, the journalist wrote that he wondered whether she had been told to say this by Lent to attract only very wealthy admirers. What he did not know was that Julia was already married.

After pressure from several colleagues, including possibly P.T. Barnum, Lent realised he had to do something about his relationship with Julia. During the European trip, he had received several requests to sell her to other showmen. It wouldn't be long before they started approaching her directly. Lent knew that he was sitting on a goldmine, and he had no plans to let her go. She was, in spite of everything, an adult, intelligent woman who might one day develop a greater sense of her financial worth than she had done up to now. He only saw one solution, even if it was rather drastic. He proposed to Julia, and she beamingly accepted. There hadn't been a single previous suitor, and she possibly believed that she would never marry. Having been billed as 'the world's ugliest woman', she could hardly believe that any man would love her, and Lent was, after all, a fine specimen, strict, determined and not too mean. He was also the single point of reference in her life. There could be no doubt about it: of course she would marry him.

Marriages within the world of freak shows were not uncommon. Many stars, including most bearded ladies, had relatively normal marriages. The man, whether deformed or not, was the traditional provider while the woman, bearded or with other remarkable features, was primarily the wife and mother. On other occasions, the stars married their managers, or even each other, though the latter were often publicity stunts, especially in the USA. Abnormally fat women tied the knot with the ultra-thin, the so-called 'human skeletons'. Female giants married male giants, and small people married each other. The publicity guaranteed larger audiences and extra income.

A prime example was the marriage of General Tom Thumb and Miss Lavinia Warren, both performers, and neither more than 32 inches high. Their real names were Charles Sherwood Stratton, born in 1838, and Mercy Lavinia Warren Bump, born in 1841. It was Barnum who gave Stratton the title 'General'. It sounded great. Barnum also thought up the name Tom Thumb. The little general soon became the public's favourite, and the money rolled in. His employer also proposed that the time was ripe to get married, and he kept a sharp eye out for a suitable short bride. He soon got word of the charming Miss Bump who appeared with a certain Miss Hardy – an 8ft-tall giantess. He sent an agent to recruit the little lady, and presented his renamed Miss Lavinia Warren as General Tom Thumb's future wife.

Despite the Civil War, there was no stopping Barnum. On 10 February 1863, the marriage preparations were in full swing. Expectations were enormous. 'Loving Lilliputians' read the giant headlines in the *New York Times*, a newspaper then of eight pages. Before the wedding, Lavinia sold photographs of herself for more than 300 dollars, and the betrothed appeared on stage right up until three days before the wedding to keep the money rolling in. And the publicity never let up, with claims like 'The 6,000 years of the world's existence has never produced her equal before'.[22] The response was so overwhelming that Barnum even suggested delaying the wedding for one month so that he could milk the commercial possibilities even further. In return, he'd pay Tom and Lavinia $15,000 dollars. A princely sum! No, said the small couple.

On the wedding day the number of invited guests to Grace Church was limited to 2,000. Many of New York's rich and powerful – governors, congressmen, generals and millionaires – turned up. President Abraham Lincoln and his wife were invited but could not come. They sent a set of exclusive Chinese folding screens as a gift, and apologised for their absence. The bridal pair later visited the Lincolns during their honeymoon tour. The Vanderbilt family sent expensive pearls, and the Astors diamond jewellery. The jewellers Tiffany honoured the couple with a silver horse and carriage, decorated with rubies. The crowds thronged the New York streets, making them impassable, and as spectators celebrated the marriage, the horrors of war were forgotten for a day. As always, the freak show was an opportunity for fantasy, an escape from reality, only this time in a setting of pomp and ceremony. A few years before, Theodore Lent had been unable to offer his bride anything like it.

Julia's wedding was strange, but not as unusual as she imagined. Almost 200 years earlier there had been a renowned hairy woman in Germany who was also proposed to by her manager. Like Julia she said yes, with the result that her husband continued to exhibit her and earn large sums. Her name was Barbara Urslerin.[23] She was born in 1629, near Augsburg, a town where Julia herself would be put on display in the 1890s, labelled as 'the most interesting woman in the world'. In her own day, Barbara was the world's most interesting woman, described in the following terms:

> . . . her very Eyebrowes were combed upwards, and all her forehead as thick and even as growes on any woman's head, neatly dress'd: There comes also two locks very long out of each ear: she had also a most prolix beard and mustachios, with long locks of haire growing on the very middle of her nose, exactly like an Iceland dog: the rest of her body not so hairy, yet exceedingly long in comparison, armes, neck, breast and back; the colour of light browne, and fine as well dressed flax.[24]

The writer was John Evelyn in his diary of 1657, after he'd seen 'the Hairy Maid', Barbara Urslerin, in a marketplace in London, on a big European tour. Evelyn wrote that he had actually seen her twenty years previously, which is probably right because Barbara had been exhibited by her parents since she was a child, and knew no other life. In 1646 she was displayed in a market in Paris, together with 'a lioness, a five-footed cow, a monstrous dolphin, an Italian water-spouter, a man without hands, a rope dancer, and a dromedary'.[25] The Frenchman Elie Brackenhoffer saw her there, and the description he wrote later about it provides fascinating material, especially since he had a special interest in the remarkable and the burlesque. He had seen many strange things, but nothing that matched Barbara. Paying extra for a private exhibition, he saw her naked. Describing her body in detail, he noted that she had round white breasts with less hair than on other parts of her body. She was a real woman, no hermaphrodite.

Johann Michael Vanbeck, who proposed to her a few years later, knew this. Marriage was not the only similarity connecting Barbara's experiences to Julia Pastrana's two hundred years later. The authorities' view of bearded ladies and their threat to public morals had hardly changed. In 1660 Barbara and her husband Johann Michael toured France, where the authorities were worried. They had had bad experiences with vulgar sideshows, and wanted guarantees that nothing would happen. In Beauvis, near Paris, Vanbeck had to apply in writing to the local bailiff, though he omitted to declare that Barbara was his wife – it made life easier. He added a copy of an elegant portrait of Barbara to emphasise that she was a respectable woman, even if she had hair on her nose. The reply said everything was in order. So he was allowed to stand in the marketplace with a tambourine, to drum up visitors to his exhibition. But the French insisted on two things: that the show had to close early in the afternoon, and more important, it must be totally respectable. That's the French: a refined nation, then and now.

On 9 August 1857, the French newspaper *L'Entr'acte*, under the heading of news and curiosities from London, wrote this: 'one thing is certain, that instead of displaying this creature, who is an insult to all propriety and decency, and who creates revulsion, one should instead shield her from all public view'.[26] The anonymous writer did not name Julia Pastrana, but, given the context, he couldn't possibly have been referring to anyone else. The French journalist had seen her on the London stage, had read Lent's exhibition pamphlet, and found the entire show utterly tasteless. He was especially upset that the brochure mentioned Julia's small, beautiful hands and feet, at the same time as writing of her mother's possible close contacts with bears and monkeys before her birth. Just what was the insinuation? Had unmentionable perversities occurred in the wilds of Mexico? The whole thing was loathsome; the Frenchman was disgusted.

Had Julia and Lent visited France? There is some evidence that they might have done, following their German tour, and that it happened on the quiet. The French were more sensitive about this kind of thing than other nations, such as the United States and England, to name but two. This was not just a matter of morals, at least not in Paris, but a matter of politics. After Napoleon III came to power in 1852, it was very important for the authorities to re-establish public law and order in a country that had just experienced its third revolution in fifty years. It was important to maintain a refined level of 'natural order' for people and society, both sociopolitically and purely biologically. There was no place for the display of grotesque monsters.

The display of such beings was, in addition, a religious problem, since many French saw freaks as the result of couplings with animals or demons. This was before Darwin's breakthrough, a time when divine power must not be questioned lest it undermine the emperor. Besides, the free-spoken Victor Hugo had recently published the poem *Fable ou Histoire* wherein Napoleon III (whom Hugo denigrates as 'Napoleon the small') is likened to an ape in a tiger suit. No wonder that an ape-woman, or *la femme-gorille*, as Julia was called by French journalists, must tread carefully in the French capital. The solution to the problem was to approach the scientific and medical societies, such as the *Société d'anthropologie de Paris* or the *Académie de médicine de Paris*, which would gladly exhibit a living monster. In this way, freaks and show people could unofficially appear in the city without the police caring or interfering. It was the masses who were dangerous, not science. After all, it would be so easy for ordinary people to be led into antisocial activities if they were exposed to perverse sideshows. Siamese twins, for example, could mislead people's thoughts; they should be banned.

Therefore the French Siamese twins, Rita-Christina, with two heads and upper bodies but a single lower torso and two legs between them, could not be displayed. The stage was denied them, both in the 1820s and 1830s. Even the world-renowned twins, Chang and Eng, from Siam (present-day Thailand) – the pair from whom the expression Siamese twins derived – received a cool welcome from the French authorities. Their career really only took off when they went to the USA as eighteen-year-olds in 1829, and it lasted for many decades. During the 1850s to 1860s, they lived in respectable surroundings, each with a wife and children. They earned good money, led pleasant, bourgeois lives with their families and toured the world as fêted celebrities. But it wasn't always that way. On their first European tour of 1828–29, they were denied entry to France. A few years later, they were allowed to slip in. Their appearance, with two independent bodies joined only at an area on their backs, seems to us quite natural. But French fastidiousness stayed alive a long time. As late as 1883 the Tocci brothers, five years old and joined in the same way as Rita-Christina, were denied the right of exhibition in Paris. But there was still a freak show in Paris, nonetheless, to the great pleasure of the French public.

I'VE GOT A BEARD, BUT I HAVE MY HONOUR

Bearded ladies were really nothing new or unheard of in French entertainment, and had been a part of it for a long time. The only difference is that they had to tread a bit more carefully in mid-century because of the turbulent times. There was a difference, though, between bearded women of Julia Pastrana's type and more feminine bearded ladies. It was easier to get the police's permission for a stage show if the woman only had a beard without hair over the rest of the body. Women with just a beard could not so easily be likened to animals, and did not threaten nature's order in the same way. They had an additional comic aspect that was disarming. The best-known French bearded lady was Catherine Delait, who was a big attraction in Lorraine at the end of the nineteenth century. She served drinks at a local watering hole, and regularly shaved. Having seen a woman with a wispy beard at a travelling carnival, she boasted that she could grow a much nicer one if she so wanted. A bet was made.

Catherine put the razor aside for good, and soon became a well-known, hirsute figure about town. After a while, she opened her own bar, *Le Café de Femme à Barbe* (the bearded lady's cafe) and sold photographs of herself. After her death, a museum opened in her honour. Catherine Delait was part of a long French tradition with different categories of artistes. There were the ordinary bearded ladies, *femmes à barbe*; there were very tall women with beards, *femmes géantes à barbe*; and last, but absolutely not least, there were *femmes colosses à barbe* – extremely fat women with beards. There were, furthermore, extremely strong women with beards, like the one sung about by Emma Valadon in her hit *La Femme à barbe* from 1864–65:[27]

> Come into my circus place,
> Nowhere else in this carnival wide
> A thing more odd than my face
> With its beard, my joy and my pride.
> Fear not to give it a shake,
> Grab hold, you'll see it's no fake,
> It'll never fall off in your hand,
> Ten centimes to see something grand.
>
> *Refrain:*
> Come every young maid and gendarme,
> And just try to bend down my arm –
> It's more easy to pull down a tree ,
> The bearded lady, that's me,
> The bearded lady, that's me.

At my birth it was commonly known
I would soon be the pride of my kin,
'Cause till now there never was grown
A beard on a young girl's chin.
By honouring me with this ornament
God gave me noble adorn-a-ment,
But I'm not an idle ingrate,
I can press a fifty stone weight.

Refrain . . .

I believe, regarding this decoration,
That men are too proud of face hair.
I'm only a woman, but my declaration
Is I'm worth six men. Ask Pierre,
Pierre the strongman over there,
A lamb as jealous as a bear –
When anyone eyes me at shows
He addles their pate with his blows.

Refrain . . .

Those garrison sergeants so valiant
Sometimes boldly offer to me
A glass of wine – they're quite gallant,
But I won't hang around the infantry.
I've my beard; I'm no blighter,
I'm a woman, no fighter –
I'll report anybody so fresh
Who neglects to respect my plump flesh

Refrain:
Come in every nursemaid and corporal,
Weak men need not pay here at all,

For my muscles like marble to see –
The bearded lady, that's me,
The bearded lady, that's me.

Julia didn't feel quite as respected when she went to Vienna in 1858 with her husband. He had no regard for her private life, she felt, constantly inviting curious scientists to examine her. Austria too had its experts, who wanted to examine the Ape-woman. But Julia was tired of it. She did not mind going on stage to sing and dance – that was her work, after all. She was most reluctant to undergo more examinations, more humiliating gropings by unfamiliar hands. She was a married woman! However, the one person in the world who should support her wouldn't hear a single word of her complaint. Unfortunately the scientists paid well and their articles doubled as free advertising. Julia could do nothing about it. New scientific examinations were conducted, and Lent sent the results to the magazine *Nationale* in 1858. The anatomical description was soon printed:

Julia Pastrana is 4½ feet high, has very broad shoulders, and has well-developed female attributes. The hands are very sweet, and the feet regular. The extremities are in all ways normal. The head is covered with thick shiny black hair, which she arranges quite tastefully; for special occasions she decorates it with feathers and flowers. Her face and entire body are covered with black hair, the nose is quite broad, the nostrils large, the lips swollen and surrounded by dark hair, the teeth irregular, the tongue a fleshy lump, chin little, ears unusually large, the eyes always strongly glazed over, expressionless.[28]

This should have been enough but Lent was adamant. He had already agreed to a meeting with an anthropology professor. His name was Herr Sigmund, and she had to present herself properly. Julia gave in. What else could she do? Herr Sigmund called the next day, and began the examination which would lead to an article in the medical journal *Wiener Medizinische Wochenschrift*. To Julia's relief, Sigmund knew that she was no monster but an informed, intelligent and friendly person. She was no dumb, half-animal thing who had learned to perform simple tricks, as Lent's brochure suggested, but a relatively satisfied young woman who could speak for herself.

When at last the learned man thanked her and left, maybe Julia felt somewhat better. Of course, only she would know how pleased she was. Just occasionally, however, something good would occur, and she would get to meet someone friendly. It wasn't often, and only very rarely did any kind of friendship develop. But it did happen once in Vienna when the famous actress and singer Friederike Gossman paid her a visit. The two women swiftly established a good rapport, exchanging experiences about their life in the footlights. Miss Gossman was surrounded by admirers, and when she later married a nobleman she became the Countess of Prokesch-Osten. Certainly, she had very different experiences from Julia regarding men and admirers. Yet they both knew that feeling of loneliness, of standing outside the community and being stared at.

How strange it was, thought the German singer, to hear Miss Pastrana speak about the world, about life and love. It was mostly through books and from her childhood that Julia knew about such things. She described her upbringing in the governor's house as close to being cut off from the world in a convent. Her adult life had also been extremely sheltered, with different managers taking pains to keep her indoors. Julia was well aware that this was typical of working in a freak show, but it didn't lessen the loneliness. When someone took Julia seriously as a person, Friederike noticed, and not as a curiosity, she came alive. Friederike was deeply touched by her sudden openness and need for closeness and by her trusting nature. Julia emphasised how much people stared at her, while few managed to see the person behind the façade. When she felt that she had reached someone who listened and respected her as an adult, intelligent individual, she felt herself become childishly elated. Julia told her that her husband, to whom she was strongly tied, 'loves me for myself!' Sometimes Julia would be almost presumptuously merry, as if she had forgotten where she was for a moment and let go of her feelings in a sudden rush. When the Countess of Prokesch-Osten was subsequently asked about Julia she had only good things to say about her. They passed many pleasant hours together. But at the same time, there seemed to be a 'light fog of sadness' which always hung over Julia.

During the Viennese stay, Julia was also visited by Hermann Otto, the German circus owner, who showed an interest in both her personality and appearance. The two had a long conversation, and Julia spoke freely of her life. Many years afterwards, Otto included Julia's story in his book about circuses and side shows, *Fahrend Volk* (*Travelling People*). 'The prototype of ugliness', he wrote about her (luckily, perhaps, Julia had died before his book was published), not because she was so much uglier than all the other freaks, but because she was perhaps the most famous hirsute person of her time. She gained a special position in people's awareness, and became almost a byword for all that was ugly and hideous. She came into the business at precisely the right time, he argued, and Lent, the 'American speculator', had made the correct move by teaching her folk songs and quaint dances. Yet Otto also felt great sympathy for the woman who had opened her heart to him.

'The poor "Miss Julia"', he wrote, before continuing his gripping narrative:

She was a monster to the whole world, an abnormality put on display for money, someone who had been taught a few artistic turns, like a trained animal. For the few who knew her better, she was a warm, feeling, thoughtful, spiritually very gifted being with a sensitive heart and mind . . . and it affected her very deeply in her heart with sadness, having to stand *beside* people, instead of *with* them, and to be shown as a freak for money, not sharing any of the everyday joys in a home filled with love. She liked to read, she was hungry for knowledge, a fine judge of persons, and besides, a good-hearted creature![29]

But the good-hearted Julia could not participate in 'happy everyday life'. She had to work for her daily bread. She had to be exhibited as and when the opportunities presented themselves, where she had novelty value. Vienna was no longer such a place. Lent appraised the market and contacted the well-known riding troupe of Renz and Hinné, arranging for Julia to perform in their coming tour of Germany. 'Horses first, horses last!' was the slogan of the famous circus director Ernst Renz, founder of Circus Renz, and one of the biggest names in European show business.

Big equestrian shows were then very popular. When not appearing in their own tent, Renz held shows inside the largest theatre halls. Lent probably got the riders to show Julia some tricks so that she could also perform on horseback besides singing, dancing, and playing the guitar and harmonica, as she had done up to now. After a few months on the road with the riders, Julia and Lent ended up in the Polish capital Warsaw, late in 1858. Julia attracted much attention and was sketched, immortalised in the theatre's ring with her husband. Lent is shown with an elegant handlebar moustache and wears a cutaway coat. He supports Julia with one hand as she stands with bow and flowers in her hair, up on the edge of the ring, while he makes an elegant gesture with his other arm. He is clearly in the process of introducing his wife, probably with a bombastic speech. Julia is clothed in a short crinoline dress, and the décolletage is generous. Perhaps it has been constructed to show hair as much as flesh. In any case, it is an unbeatable combination. A woman with a beard and lots of hair on her chest, and to top it all, from *Mexyku*, as can be read on the drawing. What a fantastic freak! Julia's face has an uncertain and thoughtful cast, and she holds up one hand expectantly to her mouth. Does she feel stared at and ridiculed? Perhaps. Is she confused or unhappy? Not necessarily. But something is about to change her life. She consummates her marriage with her husband. What new and fantastic things the future can hold!

4

The Embalmed Female Nondescript

In January 1855 the University of Moscow celebrated its 100th anniversary. From all over Russia, former students streamed into the city. The authorities expected a worthy commemoration, but things turned out differently. The prestigious university, once loyal to the Tsar and his counsellors, had now become a symbol of new, rebellious ideas. Ever since the revolutions and national uprisings of 1848, familiar to Muscovites through their newspapers, the people had been simmering. Old feudal Russia was in crisis. Ideas of freedom and self-rule were debated in taverns, despite powerful official censorship, and the nobility feared for their lives and fortunes. Simultaneously, Russia suffered great losses during the Crimean War, and it became steadily more apparent that the old regime had lost its authority. 'Russia must either fall or completely transform,'[1] wrote the young Leo Tolstoy in his diary. Since education and research could contribute to such a reformation, the University of Moscow became a centre for the new thinking. Here were the country's leading intellectuals and researchers, with ready access to invaluable scientific collections. Natural science was currently the most innovative discipline, and the University had its own Society for Natural Science. And there was a modern anatomical museum where nature's most remarkable and fantastic specimens were preserved for

future generations. Before long the museum would gain a
new specimen in its pursuit of advancing human knowledge
and enlightenment.

The winter of 1859 was a cold one. As the circus and
sideshow season drew to a close, Julia and Theodore Lent
had wandered across the continent and fetched up in
eastern Europe. They had fascinated London, shocked the
Germans and French, charmed the Austrians, and created
an uproar in Poland. In each country they had raked in the
money. Where next? In spite of the unrest in Russia, they
decided to try their luck there. The Russian circus and
theatre tradition was long and proud, and Moscow's
audiences had always appreciated a good show. Besides, in
disturbed times, the need for light entertainment was often
greater. With that thought uppermost, the Lents headed
north-east.

In Moscow, Russia's second-largest city, with almost
half a million inhabitants, their reception was rapturous.
Julia was once again the focus of popular attention, and,
man and boy, crowds flocked to her performances at the
Circus Salomansky. The spring of 1860 was one long
triumph, especially for Lent. He was now quite a wealthy
man, and the money kept pouring in. Theodore managed
the family finances, since Julia was incapable of such
things, and this did not seem to bother her. Other things
mattered more. Most of all, she wanted an experience
that was something beyond the stage of the freak show.
And this happened when, in August, Julia discovered
she was pregnant. This brought great happiness, to Julia
at least, though her husband's feelings can only be guessed
at. Would they have to carry a child with them
everywhere? But, clearly, Julia's life would change, more
than anyone could guess.

I HAVE BEEN LOVED FOR MY OWN SAKE!

> Julia Pastrana, a native of America, was delivered of a living boy at four p.m. on the 20th of March, 1860. Although the position of the child was regular, the head being turned to the left side of the pelvis, head first, yet it was necessary to make use of the forceps in order to complete the delivery, on account of the size of the infant and narrowness of the mother's pelvis. . . . The operation was carried out by Dr Chizh, assistant in the Accoucheur-Institute, aided by Accoucheur Heroldstein, of the Moscow House of Education.'[2]

Julia was a mother. Her son weighed 4kg (8½lb) and was much larger than average, especially for a mother from a small-bodied race. He had a light complexion, like his father. The head was quite large, with compressed features. Julia, very weak, rested in the hospital bed, glad that it was all over. But she soon became worried when the doctors took away the boy before she had seen him close up. She was told he was not entirely sound, but not to worry. All would be well. After a while, they came back with the child. She could hold him now, they said, but there was something they had to tell her. He was unlike other children: he had been born with hair over large parts of the body. Julia held her baby in her arms, and wept. Many years later, researchers discovered that for a carrier of the inheritable genes underlying Julia's special affliction the odds of having a normal child are 50 per cent. Julia, however, had no luck with this particular toss of a coin – but she never had been lucky.

The mother survived the delivery five and a half days, and then died of metro-peritonitis puerperalis, at midnight, between the 24th and 25th of March. The child came into the world alive, but after a little time fell into a state of asphyxia, from which it was revived by the exertions of the medical attendants; but after having lived for thirty-five hours, it died on the 22nd of March at four P.M.[3]

So read the brief, clinical description of the passing of Julia Pastrana, and her son. The boy's death was a deep blow and, it was said, she had really died of a broken heart. Certainly, she had an unusually narrow pelvis, even when compared to other women of the same height, and the child had problems coming out. But did she lose the will to live, lying there in a cold hospital half a world away from her homeland? Her child was dead. Her husband was not providing much comfort. Had she had enough of it all? No one can tell. Rumours claimed that she died with a large group of curious observers standing around the bed. 'I die happy, because I know I have been loved for my own sake!' are said to have been her last words. That sounds nice, but too good to be true. And such a myth was of no concern to the dead Julia, in any case.

Meanwhile, Lent had to start anew. A single blow had destroyed the basis of his livelihood and income. He might have grieved, might have mourned the child he would never come to know. But money, as always, had to come first. The 'nondescript', the 'baboon lady', 'la femme-gorille', Julia Pastrana the Ape-woman would be laid to rest in her grave – and how in the world would he earn a living?

But hold on – neither Julia nor their son had yet been buried. He ought not to be too hasty. Lent became acquainted through the hospital with a certain Professor Sokolov at the university. The two held secret conversations. They shared a common understanding. Two corpses, one living owner. The bodies – hairy, fascinatingly odd. One of them – famous. Business was possible!

Professor Sokolov was an expert at embalming, and had developed a special new technique, a blend of mummification and taxidermy, that resulted in a fresh and rosy, seemingly alive subject. He made the dead look as though they were living, it was claimed, without wrinkled skin or grinning death's head visages. He also had a good reputation inside anthropological and zoological circles. Lent had never heard of him, but after all he was no expert in this area. On the other hand, he knew a good deal when he saw one. Things had to be carried out quickly. Four days had already passed since Julia's death, and the corpses were no longer fresh. One thing was certain, no burial would be paid for until every other approach had been tried. Professor Sokolov proved to be salvation. A detailed contract was hastily written, signed by the university representatives, the American consul of the city, and by Theodore Lent.

'The dead bodies were sent to be embalmed in the theatre of Moscow University, with a view to their being preserved in the Anatomical Museum of that University,' wrote Sokolov in an article in the *Lancet*.[4] Science had finally got hold of Julia Pastrana.

The preparation of the dead is an ancient art that can be performed in many ways for many different motives, be they religious, scientific, political or ideological. And don't, of course, underestimate purely economic justifications. The best known examples of this worldwide process are the Egyptian mummies, saved for eternity for reasons of religion and power politics. Already in the fifth century BC, Herodotus, 'the father of history', had described the Egyptians' ancient embalming technique. Herodotus had travelled widely in his younger years, throughout the Greek world, Egypt and parts of Africa, making thorough observations of everything he saw. In his famous *Histories* he gives accounts of three different embalming methods used by the Egyptians.

The most exclusive, reserved for the richest customers, consisted of the deceased's brain being drawn out through the nostrils with the help of an inserted metal hook. Afterwards, a cut was made in the side of the body and the internal organs removed. The abdominal cavity was cleansed and washed, first with palm wine and afterwards with a special mixture of spices. The corpse was then filled with myrrh and other aromatic ingredients, and sewn up. Afterwards, it was placed in natron[5] for seventy days and regularly washed before being wrapped in bandages. Finally, it was placed in a wooden coffin set against the wall of the grave chamber.

The second method was less delicate, and was used for those of lower status. No cuts were made in the body, and no intestines were removed. Instead, large amounts of oil of cedar were injected through the anus which was afterwards blocked. The body was then pickled in natron for the usual seventy days, before the oil of cedar was drained out. By that time, all the interior organs and flesh had dissolved, and ran out with the remaining oil. Only skin and bones remained, and the process was over. Finally, writes Herodotus, 'the corpse was handed over to the family without further ado'.

The third method, used for embalming the poor, simply involved removing the intestines quickly by means of a purge, before pickling the body in natron as usual. Herodotus is kind enough to tell us that rich, beautiful or famous women were not handed over for embalming for at least three to four days after death – to prevent unmentionable violations by the embalmers.

Several thousand years later, more than sixty years after Julia Pastrana's death, Russian – now Soviet – embalmers had a new and greater challenge tossed into their laps. 'Kings are embalmed because they are kings,' the chief of the Soviet security police declared in January 1923.[6] No other rationale was necessary when the communist leaders, with Stalin at their head, decided to preserve the remains of Vladimir Ilich Ulyanov – better known as Lenin – for posterity. A cult would be formed. Like mummified pharaohs and kings given eternal life, the idea of great Lenin would live forever, symbolised by his embalmed body.

Only one person disagreed, Lenin's widow, who wrote in *Pravda*, immediately following her husband's death in 1924:

> Comrades, workers, and farmers, I have an important request to make of you. Do not let your pain be transformed into demonstrations of adoration for Vladimir Ilich's personality. Do not put up buildings or monuments in his name. When he was alive he set little store by such things; indeed, he actively disliked them.'[7]

She was, of course, ignored. The Communist Party's leadership had decided that Lenin should be preserved for the good of the people and the party, and that was that. The task was far from simple. No one was willing to take total responsibility. Speed was essential since the corpse's skin was beginning to wrinkle, and was turning an unpleasant dark colour. Six litres of a mixture of formaldehyde, alcohol and glycerin were injected into the main artery as a temporary measure. Much of this ran out again, and the body was about to dry up. A committee was established to deal with the problem: it proclaimed that long-term preservation of corpses was an impossibility.

A Ukrainian professor of anatomy called Vorobyev got wind of this, and dismissed the committee's pronouncements as pure rubbish. Of course bodies can be preserved, he said, for as long as is necessary. Many examples could be cited. Julia Pastrana's name was not mentioned, but Professor Vorobyev must have known about the work of his colleague, the now-deceased Sokolov. Another committee proposed freezing Lenin's remains, but Vorobyev insisted it was a bad idea. Freezing would destroy the cells, and keeping a constant low temperature was not easy, he argued. Vorobyev was now recruited into the embalming work against his will; he had no other choice than to do his best. He told a co-worker: 'As for me, I don't want to suffer the fate of those alchemists who undertook to embalm Pope Alexander VI. They had themselves paid a great deal of money but they were so inept that they destroyed the body and had to flee for their lives.'[8]

While powerful high priests in ancient Egypt had carried out the mummification process, and leading scientific researchers of the 1800s had dominated the art of embalming, conditions in what had formerly been Russia were quite different after 1917. Professor Vorobyev and his colleagues were totally dependent on the Communist Party's favour, and the embalming of Lenin became a perilous undertaking. 'I'm more worried about the living than about the dead in all this,' said one of those involved.[9]

Before beginning the secondary embalming, the final and terminal process, the body was dipped into a bath of glycerin and potassium acetate. After that immersion, the intestines were removed and the abdominal cavity thoroughly rinsed. Formaldehyde was injected into those areas of the body that had decayed most, before the corpse was once again immersed in a 3 per cent formaldehyde solution. Because this was not good enough to prevent dissolution, the corpse was taken out of the bath and opened up again.

Many large incisions were made to give the chemicals better access, and the embalming fluid was changed. Alcohol, glycerin and potassium acetate were now added, and the amount of formaldehyde was increased. That helped, and the corpse's skin became more moist and elastic. Unsightly dark spots on the face and hands were removed, along with mould and other signs of decay. The mouth and eyes were sewn shut again, after the insertion of glass eyes to prevent the eye sockets from appearing hollow. With that, the task was complete; it was time to await the verdict.

As things turned out, there was nothing to worry about. 'I'm very moved. . . . It takes my breath away. He looks as he did when we saw him a few hours after he died – perhaps even better.' So said Lenin's brother on viewing the embalmed corpse.[10] Vorobyev and his helpers could breathe easier.

Ten years later, an American scientist visiting the Lenin mausoleum in Moscow expressed his admiration: 'The embalming of Lenin is the most perfect example I've ever seen of the art – better even than the mummies of ancient Egypt. Don't the Soviet scientists say Vladimir Ilich's body will be preserved for all eternity, without ever suffering the ravages of time?'[11] Almost the same thing had been said about Julia Pastrana, ten years before Lenin was born, in the same city, and in the same condition as the dead dictator.

VISUALLY AESTHETIC

The morbid embalming routine described by Sokolov would make Julia more famous than ever:

When the body of the child was embalmed, it was still fresh, and exhibited scarcely any signs of decomposition, except a slight smell and a dullness in the corneae of the eyes. The mother's body, on the contrary, was in a far less perfect state of preservation, and signs of rapid decomposition were plainly visible, especially in the intestinal organs. The whole of the skin was of a dusky colour; some parts of the body were slightly distended, and emitted a putrid smell. The belly was somewhat inflated, and of a greenish hue; when tapped, it gave a drum-like sound. There was a slight flow of reddish fluid from the mouth, and still more from the nostrils.

Such was the state of the body when I began to embalm it, or rather to preserve it, by injection of decay-arresting mixtures to halt the decay. As soon as they were introduced into the body its dark parts began to whiten; the spots where corruption had already set in recovered their normal condition, and after a little time became remarkably firm, especially where the solutions had been most successfully applied; and the disagreeable smell ceased. Notwithstanding every precaution, some of the vessels of the uterus were torn in the operation; and there was difficulty in getting the preserving fluids through the capillary vessels, arising from the distance from the heart. This unfortunate occurrence, which often happens when subjects are being injected for anatomical purposes, delayed the process of embalmment, and I was obliged to inject several parts of the body successively. The body of the child did not give rise to equal difficulties, as it was in a fresher state when the embalming began, and immediately after the injections took effect, it grew firm in every part.[12]

The professor was proud of his work. What was special in the case of Julia and her son was how natural they looked, and how Sokolov had managed to give them a natural facial and bodily appearance. That was particularly so in the case of the mother, since the baby was mounted in a standing position on a rod – 'like a parrot', as someone later remarked. The boy did, however, have an alert expression and almost looked alive. That was most important. He was clad in a sweet little dress.

As for Julia, the professor had posed her in an active and dynamic position. She stood with her arms slightly out from her sides, hands placed emphatically on her hips. She wore her finest embroidered silk dress. She had a string of pearls with a cross around her throat, and precious stones and feathers in her upswept hair. Her feet were firmly planted apart, her stance self-assured. The head was half turned to the left. The facial expression was open, determined and clear-eyed. The overall impression was that of a self-confident, proud woman. It might be thought that she was confronting something, perhaps the public who stood and stared at her, or the world in general, which had so rarely offered her anything other than toil and sorrow. Julia embalmed, in other words, appeared precisely as the living woman never did. It was a paradox that few perceived and that mattered to no one. What was paramount was that the resemblance was remarkable and that the body was an aesthetically pleasing spectacle – for a corpse.

When the mummies were put on display in the university's anatomical museum, they were a minor scientific sensation. Never before had anyone seen such lifelike results, and their reputation spread rapidly throughout the European scientific community. When a paleontological expedition from St Petersburg set out on a long journey the same year, it went via Moscow just to see the preserved bodies. More researchers came to the city to admire Sokolov's handicraft. Julia was the pride of the museum, but the management could not relax – Lent was waiting in the wings, about to strike.

Sokolov described the subsequent events:

The two bodies were embalmed by me about six months ago with a view to their being permanently preserved in the anatomical museum at the University of Moscow. But as the mother and child belonged during their lifetime to an American subject, a contract was drawn up by the American consul before the bodies were sent to the anatomical theatre, in accordance with which they have been both taken away again by the American husband of Pastrana. This American deposited a legal certificate of his marriage with Julia Pastrana, attested by the consul, in order to prove his right to take away the embalmed bodies. The bodies of these two individuals – one of which has been the subject of general curiosity – well deserved a place among the rarities in this museum, and wherever they may be they have a claim upon the scientific world.[13]

Lent thought he had cut a good deal selling his wife and child to the university. Unconfirmed sources suggest a price of £500 sterling. Not a bad price for goods normally considered to be unmarketable. But Lent had a trick up his sleeve, having arranged for an escape clause in the contract with the museum. As the nearest kin and previous owner, he could buy back the mummies at a later point. And that point was when he saw, six months later, how extraordinarily well they looked. He couldn't have dreamed of that beforehand, even though the contract showed he took no chances. It is rumoured that Lent had to part with the equivalent of £800 for the return of the bodies. Sokolov had performed a major piece of work, and worried about the loss to research, while the museum demanded compensation for its loss. Lent paid without complaint, and regained control over Julia. And he was together again with his stuffed first-born, standing obediently on its perch. The family was reunited. The curtain could go up once more.

. . . THIS FANTASTIC PHENOMENON OF NATURE

Trade in dead freaks was then neither unusual nor unheard of, at least not in show business, nor in the world of research. The corpses of remarkable people were stolen and sold, dissected and mummified. Sometimes, the transactions and operations were planned while the subject was still alive. Freaks were not primarily people; they were perambulating investments. The best and most fantastic therefore were not allowed to die and to be buried without further ado. That would be letting money slip through your fingers. Some proposed a scientific justification about valuable anthropological material. And so people went 'over their dead bodies' to get hold of anatomical curiosities, even before Julia's time.

John Hunter, born in 1728, was one of Great Britain's best known doctors. He is seen now as a pioneer in British surgery, and as a near genius in most branches of biology. He was also an eager collector of biological material. At the time of his death his own private museum contained over 13,000 pieces. There were skeletons of extinct giant animals, the remains of such exotic and unusual creatures as elephants and giraffes, and innumerable rare beasts preserved in spirit. Hunter himself had dissected over 500 animal species, many of them from his own zoo, including leopards, wolves, zebras, bats and ostriches.

Most notably, the museum housed a unique collection of anthropological material. Hunter was not an idle man, and the collection of human remains was one of his abiding interests. There they stood, either in alcohol, or in glass cases, or displayed in other ways, for example as cleanly picked, carefully mounted skeletons. One still stands in the museum today two centuries later.[14]

In 1761, a special male child was born in a small Irish

town. Baptised Charles Byrne, he was later best known as the Irish Giant. Charles grew quickly, and even as a young man was over 8 feet tall. He was thought then to be the tallest person in the world. All his family were of normal height, and it was thought that his enormous growth had been caused by his being conceived on top of a giant haystack. Regardless of the reason, everyone was certain that Charles should use his height to his best advantage, especially since his intellect wasn't his strongest card. Show business was the obvious vocation.

In the spring of 1782 Charles travelled to London to be exhibited:

However striking a curiosity may be, there is generally some difficulty in engaging the attention of the public; but even this was not the case with the modern living Colossus, or wonderful Irish Giant, for no sooner was he arrived at an elegant apartment at the cane shop in Spring Gardens, next door to Cox's Museum, than the curious of all degrees resorted to see him, being sensible that a prodigy like this never made its appearance among us before, and the most penetrating have frankly declared, that neither the tongue of the most florid orator or pen of the most ingenious writer, can sufficiently describe the elegance, symmetry and proportion of this wonderful phenomenon in Nature, and that all description must fall infinitely short of giving that satisfaction which may be obtained on a judicious inspection.[15]

The curious spectators included the elegant figure of John Hunter. Charles Byrne was not acquainted with the famous surgeon, nor his scientific museum. Perhaps that was just as well. Hunter, for his part, had seen something he wanted. If the 21-year-old giant on the podium had been able to read

the doctor's thoughts, he would have turned away in fear
and loathing. Hunter kept a close eye on Byrne, and waited
for a suitable opportunity to strike. He didn't have to wait too
long. Byrne had problems and began to drink too much, his
health declined and his money disappeared. Just one year
after the success in London he was considerably weakened,
despite his youth. This 'truly amazing phenomenon,
indisputably the most extraordinary production of the
human species ever beheld since the days of Goliath'[16] was
in a bad way, and the vultures gathered. Soon Byrne's house
in Cockspur Street was almost surrounded by the hired
agents of various scientific researchers. All were after one
thing, the giant's mortal remains, and they didn't hide the
fact. Wherever he went, the sick Byrne was shadowed by
those waiting to get hold of his corpse. He resented this
fiercely. In the end, he took the step of paying for his own
burial, and reached an agreement with the undertaker that
his body be buried as soon as possible out in the open sea. He
furthermore hired several tough minders to watch over his
sickbed, and paid some fishermen to ship the coffin out to
sea. This, he hoped, would give him not only peace of mind
but also peace in death.

But John Hunter was one step ahead of him. Hunter's
men bribed the bodyguards and fishermen and plied them
with drink. A few hours after Byrne's death, they removed
his corpse. Hunter had rigged up an enormous cooking pot
at home, into which the giant was stuffed. The Irish Giant
was boiled for hours, until the flesh had softened and
loosened from the bones. Afterwards, the bones were
scraped clean and bleached, and were finally mounted in a
standing position. So Hunter got his skeleton, and the
London museum became one attraction richer. Ethically,
Hunter had no problem, and slept well. Science had to use
all available means; sentiment was irrelevant. The treatment

of the remains of the dead made no difference to *them*, regardless of whether they are boiled or embalmed. Any real professional knew that.

Which brings us to the zoologist Francis Buckland. In February 1862, he was thumbing through his newspaper when he suddenly noticed an advertisement for an exhibition newly arrived in London. 'The Embalmed Female Nondescript', read the heading. Buckland sat up. An embalmed female curiosity? Displayed with her own child? He went down to the Burlington Gallery, 191 Piccadilly, where the exhibition was being held,[17] with his friend Mr Bartlett, a highly respected taxidermist and preparator at the British Museum. Approaching the stiff, skirt-clad mummy, Buckland stopped suddenly and exclaimed, 'Julia Pastrana!' Yes, he was sure now, it was definitely her, the woman he had met five years previously. The suspicion had already crossed his mind that the embalmed nondescript might be Julia – after all, hirsute women described as 'the nondescript' were rather rare.

But he had not imagined that it really would be Julia herself, because the world of freak shows was notorious for its lies and exaggerations. Some unscrupulous showman might well have simply stolen Julia's sobriquet without giving rise to any public comment. But this was the one and only Julia Pastrana before his eyes, as fantastic as ever, even in her deceased state.

A dark-haired, middle-aged man heard Buckland's exclamation and walked over. He presented himself as Mr Lent, the exhibition's owner and Pastrana's former manager, and proposed a closer examination for the two learned gentlemen. Bartlett had never seen such highly skilled mummifications, not in the British Museum, nor indeed anywhere else.

Buckland described Julia in great detail:

The figure was dressed in the ordinary exhibition costume used in life, and placed erect upon a table. The limbs were by no means shrunken or contracted, the arms and chest, &c. retaining their former roundness and well-formed appearance. The face was marvellous; exactly like an exceedingly good portrait in wax, but it was *not* formed in wax. The closest examination convinced me that it was the true skin, prepared in some wonderful way; the huge deformed lips and the squat nose remained exactly as in life; and the beard and luxuriant growth of soft black hair on and about the face were in no respect changed from their former appearance.[18]

Lent was no less enthusiastic. Playing the scientific card with an adman's skill, he placed a new announcement in *The Illustrated London News*:

JULIA PASTRANA EMBALMED
This example of modern embalming, by a new and hitherto unknown process, has been critically examined by many of the leading scientific men in London, declared by them to be the most fantastical and uniquely successful case of embalming ever carried out.[19]

The *Lancet* on 15 March that year published a smaller article, entitled 'A new process of embalming and preserving the human body'. Julia Pastrana and her son could now be seen at no. 191 Piccadilly; they were enthusiastically described as 'this remarkable result of modern science'. 'The exhibition is an extraordinary one', the article emphasised, and urged all interested parties to visit the result of this 'completely successful system' in the treatment of dead individuals.

But sensationalism only has a limited lifespan, and a short while later the 'fantastical and unique' exhibition was on the road again. The year after Buckland's visit, the Lent family – adult and child, living and dead – was on an extensive tour of Germany. Julia was now advertised as the 'Original Mummy' and as the 'World's Most Interesting Woman'. Later, she and her son were incorporated into a German cabinet of anatomical monstrosities, being trundled about in carts all over Europe. With Lent trailing along, the Germans travelled as far north as Sweden, and Julia showed that she could still draw them in.

Of course, it wasn't like the times when she sang and danced with fresh flowers in her hair. Now she required regular dusting, even though she was kept on display in a locked glass case.

But what effect did all this have on Lent? 'He let the entire world share his sorrow. That is to say, he exhibited his wife and child in a glass case for money' – so wrote the showman Hermann Otto, some years later.[20] With staring eyes and silent accusation, Julia gave her husband much to mull over, and the effects on him were clear after a few years. Perhaps he already saw what the future held. He began to tire of it all, after almost ten years on the road with his wife. In the end he hired Julia out to a privately owned English cabinet of curiosities. Some years later, he received a better offer from a museum in Vienna, and once again Julia visited the familiar surroundings of her earlier fame. One can only wonder whether Friederike Gossmann, now Countess Prokesch-Osten, might have paid her a visit?

One sensitive soul who did go to see her was Hermann Otto. One rainy evening, he walked into a tent in *Praüscher's Volkmuseum* in Vienna.

I came with possessive feelings before that glass case, that *coffin*, where that lifeless body was shown . . . and very many thoughts came over [me] when [I] saw the mummy.

She stood before me in a red, silk-like harlot's dress with a frightening rictus across her face, with her child in a similar costume on a pole beside her like a parrot. The rain streamed down outside between the show-booths. . . . And a heavy wind howled round the tent, and I felt a deep, deep sympathy for that poor corpse who could not see and hear, nor feel pain and sorrow. I remembered her saying once with a happy smile, 'He loves me for my own sake.'[21]

So Otto described his meeting with Julia many years after her death, under the chapter-heading 'Hairy and Bearded People' in his book *Travelling Folk*. Otto was the first writer who actually took an interest in Julia's fate, and who tried to garner details about her life. For all its limitations, this was a rare account that took a humane perspective, in which Otto revealed his sympathy for Julia and recognised the tragedy of her situation; and this showed more insight than any of the previous scientific descriptions of Julia. Otto's account closes with these words:

What eventually happened to the mummies of mother and child – did they find quiet in a dusty corner of a museum, or are they still on the road in some travelling show's tent? Who knows? I only know that the woman who died in Moscow in 1860 was with her child in the anthropological display of J.B. Gassner in Munich in 1889. And that this was alongside another Pastrana, alive, who called herself Miss Zenora Pastrana.[22]

5

An Extremely Remarkable Hairiness

In the Bohemian city of Karlsbad in the early 1870s there lived a young girl named Marie Bartel. She was her family's great shame, and her stern, well-to-do father kept her indoors most of the time. On the streets, she was teased and pestered because she'd been born with hair over large parts of her body, and a thick beard grew on her chin. However, it was not until her confirmation that she was shaved for the first time. Her face had gross masculine features with narrow eyes, heavy eyebrows and a broad nose. The popular explanation was that her mother had been frightened by a shaggy dog while pregnant. Being Marie wasn't easy, even though she grew up to be a normal young woman. She was headstrong and intelligent, and received a good education. She read and wrote several languages, and was a good conversationalist.

One warm autumn day, she was sitting alone in the garden, reading. Without any warning someone threw a paper bag over the garden wall. Curious, Marie opened it and found sweet, delicious plums. Going to the wall, she peered over to see a good-looking man smiling at her. With an elegant bow, he lifted his hat and presented himself, speaking with a noticeable foreign accent. Marie smiled and blushed under her beard.

Soon the stranger paid a formal visit to Marie's father, the respected businessman Herr Bartel. Over drinks in his office,

Marie's future was discussed and sealed in the space of a few hours. After they had come out again, and the guest had bid farewell, Marie was told. She was engaged, and was going to be married, as soon as possible. Then she would leave the city, and maybe even the country, for that matter. Saints be praised, was her father's attitude. Marie was probably pleased enough, even though this had all happened at lightning speed. She was not exactly spoiled for suitors, and the man with the plums was attractive and elegant, even though relatively old, being fifty or more. But according to her father, he had money, most importantly, and was by the way, an American, in the entertainment business. His name? Theodore Lent.

Herr Bartel was initially sceptical about the stranger who had suddenly appeared and asked for his daughter's hand. No one knows how Lent persuaded Bartel or how much money, if any, he offered. But it seems unlikely that money, possibly quite an amount, did not play its part in striking the deal. And Marie's father had his terms: the couple must leave Karlsbad immediately after the wedding, and preferably keep away thereafter. Since Bartel knew Lent's occupation, he made Lent promise never to put his wife on display for money. Bartel was happy to get rid of her, hairy disgrace that she was, but there were limits. Marie must never set foot on stage, under any circumstance. Of course not, Lent said. As if anyone would ever show off his own wife. Seriously, in all honesty, Lent could never be a party to anything of the sort.

The two lovebirds were soon well and truly married and shortly afterwards they left town. Marie possessed little, but Theodore said he would buy her whatever she needed, together with fine clothes and pretty dresses. And he kept his promise, just as he had in making an early departure from Karlsbad. When he bought her fine formal dresses with deep decolletage, Marie thought it almost too good to be true. She soon understood why: Theodore had plans.

One day he came into their hotel room with something to tell her: he had decided to allow Marie to perform on stage. Just a bit to begin with, for the fun of it. She could sing a few folk melodies, dance a little, and then see what she thought. To Theodore's pleasure, Marie agreed to give it a go. There was one small extra detail: if she was going to go on stage perhaps Marie ought to change her name – something a bit more foreign and exotic. How about Pastrana, for example – Zenora Pastrana? Sounds nice, doesn't it? Yes, Marie was happy with that. She agreed to start singing lessons immediately. But first, they had to visit Vienna to get something from a carnival. Or rather, someone.

A short while later, they were all together: Lent and his young bride Marie – now known as Zenora – with Julia Pastrana and her son. One can hardly imagine Marie's reaction on being presented to her stuffed predecessor. Or to her mummified stepson. Who knows what she really thought? All we do know is that she soon accepted the bizarre logic of the freak show, and that the four of them went back on the road. This readiness to get on with things was essential to surviving in such a rough trade; and after a while Marie developed a good head for business and money.

Marie appeared on stage with Julia and the son in the background in their glass case. Lent introduced her as Julia's younger sister. Good business, yes, but psychologically appalling for Marie. Increasingly she felt as if Julia's eyes were staring at the back of her neck just when she was in the middle of her song and dance routine. Nervous and unwell, she began to forget her lines. She told Lent that she could not continue like this. Begone, ye dead! Lent was understanding and they decided to hire out the mummies. Julia and son returned to the carnival in Vienna, and the

married couple continued their grand tour of Europe. Lent,
however, tried occasionally to present Marie as the deceased
Julia. Marie no doubt found this unpleasant but, this being
show business, agreed. Like Julia, Marie learned to appear
on horseback. She was a great success, appearing in front of
large crowds in many countries.

Hermann Otto witnessed Marie's talents:

. . . this woman displayed a very remarkable hirsuteness.
The still living, as of this day, 33-year-old Zenora is an
elegant creature in her movements. It is only through
her facial form and the abnormal growth of hair over
her entire body, with the exception of her breast, that she
differs from other members of her sex. She is in addition
extremely clever at womanly skills, has mastered several
languages, and is also musically gifted. Eyewitnesses
agree that she has developed an admirable gracefulness
while dancing, and to put it directly, she has danced her
way into the hearts of the spectators. This is why she
isn't a spinster.[1]

Otto's soberly enthusiastic description is quite comprehensive.
And Marie was a remarkable woman, and not just because of
her hairiness. In contrast to the naïve, homeless Julia, Marie
was strong and self-assured. She could exert control over her
husband, who was by then feeling his age. He had lived a
strenuous life, always on the road, never at rest. He had been a
wanderer all his days, in an endless procession of trains and
horse carts, and crossed the Atlantic on several occasions.

As late as 1875, Lent's name turns up in New York as the
temporary director of the city's only permanent circus. This
may have been a trip to his home country together with
Marie, while she performed and he directed the circus for a
season or two. Perhaps Julia stayed on in Europe, but she

had not been forgotten after her previous triumphal tour of the United States. She was no longer in the news but was now a symbol of ugliness, being used as the image of the ape-man, the Missing Link that Darwin had proposed in 1871 in his book *The Descent of Man*, which had generated controversy on both sides of the Atlantic.

The link with Darwin is pertinent because in 1871, the same year that Darwin mentioned Julia in another of his books, the New York readers of *Appleton's Journal* could find, under the heading 'A Case in Point', the following paragraph:

A splendid illustration of Mr Darwin's theory has turned up in Vienna. There is a girl there, aged thirteen, a native of Palermo, Thérèse Gambardella, who is literally covered with hair so thickly that the Vienna papers pronounce her skin more like a fur than anything else. The famous Julia Pastrana is described as perfectly smooth compared with the new claimant to celebrity, whose hairy covering extends from head to foot, even the forehead – which in similar cases is said to have been invariably found bare – being entirely overgrown. The head closely resembles that of a monkey, and several abnormalities in the build of the body still further complete the resemblance. We do not hear whether the young lady is graced with a tail, but the shape of her jaws and teeth, the pliability of her tongue – which she can roll up completely in her mouth – her excellent appetite, her restlessness, etc., strikingly remind one of the agile and amusing animals in the Zoological Gardens. Signorina Gambardella's intellectual capacity is said to correspond with her prepossessing exterior.[2]

Inherited traits and animal-like ancestors were not discussed only in newspapers and scientific journals; literature also took up the theme, making the ape-man an

example of the utmost hideousness. Charles Reade, the
novelist and playwright, had several characters discuss
Reginald, the wild boy of a titled British family, in his 1872
novel, *A Terrible Temptation*.[3] Reginald climbs trees all day,
even though he is musical and can talk, and is nicknamed
'the little monster'. How can ordinary, civilised Sir Charles
and Lady Bassett bear offspring like this, they wonder. One
character, the writer Mr Rolfe, a thinly disguised version of
the author, explains, having closely examined the boy: 'I see
what naturalists call a reversion in race; a boy who
resembles in colour and features neither of his parents, and
indeed, bears little resemblance to any of the races that
have inhabited England since history was written. He
suggests rather some Oriental type.'[4]

In spite of the child's parents being shocked by such a
claim, Rolfe continues:

'I don't undertake to account for it, with any precision.
How can I? Perhaps there is Moorish blood in your family
and here it has revived; you look incredulous, but there
are plenty of examples, ay, and stronger than this; every
child that is born resembles some progenitor; how then
do you account for Julia Pastrana, a young lady who
dined with me last week, and sang me "Ah perdona,"
rather feebly, in the evening. Bust and figure like any
other lady, hands exquisite, arms neatly turned, but with
long silky hair from the elbow to the wrist. Face, ugh!
forehead made of black leather, eyes all pupil, nose an
excrescence, chin pure monkey, face all covered with
hair; briefly, a type extinct ten thousand years before
Adam, yet it could revive at this time of day. Compared
to La Pastrana, and many much weaker examples of
antiquity revived, that I have seen, your Mauritanian son
is no great marvel after all.'[5]

The boy's mother objects that his nurse Mary, being dark-skinned, must be largely at fault. Sir Charles, for his part, points out that the boy 'talks and feels precisely like an English snob',[6] and the discussion continues on that level.

Reade, who was particularly interested in human society, accumulated a large library of sociological and anthropological material, and must have met Julia Pastrana in London in 1857. He used her as literary material after Darwin's theories made her topical again. Ape-women were always good material.

Back in Europe, no one likened Marie Bartel to an ape. She was too feminine for that, despite her rough and bearded face. She was taller than Julia, slimmer, and more elegant; but she was something absolutely special and people gladly paid to see her. Marie and Lent toured for almost ten years, with particular success in England and France. Around 1880 Lent and Marie bought themselves a little wax museum in St Petersburg, where he had contacts from his earlier tours, and decided to retire. Conditions were then quieter in Russia, with Tsar Alexander ruling for many years in a liberal fashion. Then, in 1881, he was murdered by extremists, and his successor initiated more restrictive domestic and foreign policies.

The Lents noticed little of this, being comfortably established in one of the country's largest cities. They were part of the upper class, with a fat bank account, and viewed the future with rosy eyes. And they had a son, a handsome, blonde little boy without a single abnormal hair on his body. Julia was stashed away in a distant carnival, and Marie had her own family and no longer needed to perform. She deserved a rest, and, besides, she was no longer the most famous of her kind.

. . . A MOTHER, WHO HELD A CHILD IN HER ARMS

The 12 May 1883 issue of *La Nature* described the following:

> A little girl of seven years, called Krao, completely covered by hair and with additional ape-like features, is now being shown in the Aquarium at Westminster, in London. Her whole body is decked with straight, glistening hair; the face is sui generis with a jutting jaw; she has the ability to stretch her lips almost as far forward as a chimpanzee, the grimaces when she is irritated are characteristic of chimpanzees; she also has prehensile toes that she uses to pluck up quite small objects from the ground. With these features one might say that she has to be a middle link between humans and apes, 'the missing link' for which man has fruitlessly hunted so long. But that she is absolutely not. Monsieur Keane, the learned anthropologist who has studied this remarkable specimen, reports that she without doubt is a member of the genus Homo.[7]

The little girl Krao certainly was human, in spite of some people's doubts. She was born in Indo-China, in what later became Laos, and was brought to England by the Great Farini, one of Europe's foremost showmen. Farini claimed that Krao and her family had been held prisoner by the King of Burma, and that Farini's own agents had got them out. Krao belonged to a tribe of extraordinary ape people who lived high up in the trees, and lived on raw meat and rice. Farini said that he had personally received permission from the Burmese royal family to take the girl to England and adopt her as his own daughter. And he topped this by claiming that she was an example of Darwin's missing link.

Little Krao soon became the new star in the freak show

firmament, and Farini toured with her in England, Germany, America and France. The French authorities were, as usual, difficult, and in 1883 Krao and her family were denied entry to the country. Three years later they were allowed in provided that they keep a low profile. Farini resolved the matter by hiring a private room, where he held small exhibitions in a discreet fashion from two to six in the afternoon, and from eight to eleven in the evening. This aroused little attention in the press, even though French researchers turned out in force to see the fantastic ape person. After the show, most agreed that Krao was actually human. Nevertheless, she was a great sensation, not least on account of Farini's excellent promotional skills. Krao remained in show business for many years and ended up as one of the century's best-known hairy freaks. Zenora Pastrana could not compete with a missing link from Indochina. It was time for her to retire.

Marie and Lent had a few easy years in Saint Petersburg but then he began to behave strangely, becoming forgetful, anxious and hysterical. Eventually, things got really bad: one day in 1884 he was found in his underclothes on a bridge across the River Neva. He was jumping and dancing around, shrieking incomprehensibly and ripping banknotes into bits, chucking them into the water. Everyone stopped and watched. They shook their heads and smiled. What was wrong with this man, they wondered, shouting in a foreign language, acting like a madman?

Lent became a public spectacle for a short while and became himself a shocking, amusing curiosity. No one knew his background or the cause of his madness, or even cared. Did his previous life and deeds haunt him? Did he have vague memories of a young woman who once said she loved him, who gave birth to his child, whom he had handed over to a taxidermist, to be made into a grinning corpse? Solely so that he could earn the money he was now casting into the swirling waters of the Neva? Whatever the causes may have been, Marie acted promptly, and had him forcibly committed to an asylum for the insane, where he died soon after.

By 1888 Marie had had enough of cold Russia, and, longing for home, decided to return to Germany. There was nothing to keep her in St Petersburg, with her husband and now her son dead (at the age of seven). On the way home she stopped in Munich to pick up the two bodies she had inherited from Lent. They had been shown in many different places over the years, and had provided a decent income. Now she wanted to be rid of them. However, she decided to put them on display for one last time, in the premises of the Anthropological Society of Munich. And by appearing there in person at the same time, she took the opportunity to kill the rumour that she and Julia were the same person, as Lent had sometimes claimed.

Afterwards, she allowed J.B. Gassner, who had previously exhibited the mummies, to take permanent possession of them. She was present several times during the period of the exhibition, and it was there she was seen by Hermann Otto. She took no fee, apparently, having earned enough from the dead, and travelled back to Karlsbad. By now her mother was dead, and her father was very old. Since he needed household help – or so it is claimed – he welcomed her back, but Marie was not going to be exploited any longer. She moved to Dresden and bought a house. A few years later, she found a husband twenty years younger than herself. She dressed in men's clothes, shaved daily, and always went out wearing a veil. She died in 1900.

Meanwhile, Julia was still on the move. The enterprising Gassner wanted to milk her for all she was worth, and exhibited her at a number of German fairs. In 1895, at a big circus convention in Vienna, he was given a good offer

The view from Sierra de Huehuerachi in north-west Mexico. Espinosa and Julia were said to have survived in wild mountain areas like these for a long period.

Julia Pastrana, drawn from life, probably in London in 1857.

Above: P.T. Barnum. Below: The elephant on the poster, the world's largest in captivity, was bought by Barnum from the London Zoo for $10,000, causing great resentment in England since the animal was famous and loved. Most people, the press, and even Queen Victoria got involved but 'Jumbo', as Barnum named him, soon became the greatest circus attraction in the USA.

Drawing of Julia, 1895.

A friendly orang-utan, from 1812. In the spirit of Rousseau and the Enlightenment the orang-utan began to be seen as a human-like, benign creature at the start of the 1800s. A few decades later, these large primates were regarded as frightful monsters, as they had been before the Enlightenment.

The unrestrained atmosphere at the so-called 'penny theatres' of Victorian London. The scene below dates from 1857, the year of Julia's arrival in England.

Bearded insane women, colourfully described in *Medical Curiosities*,1896.

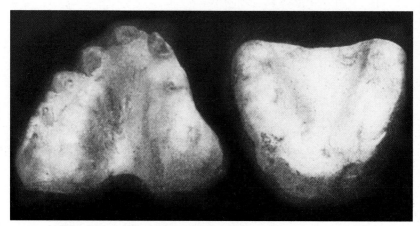

Left to right, Julia's upper and lower palates. These casts are in the Odontological Museum of the Royal College of Surgeons in London. The syndrome is called gingivial hyperplasia – overdeveloped gums.

The only known photograph – much retouched – of Julia
taken while she was still alive.

Julia as portrayed by the artist H. König in Gartenlaube.
The facial features are exaggerated and caricatured.

Barbara Urslerin was known for her beautiful harpsichord playing. People with her special form of hirsuteness are thought to have been the basis of the werewolf legend.

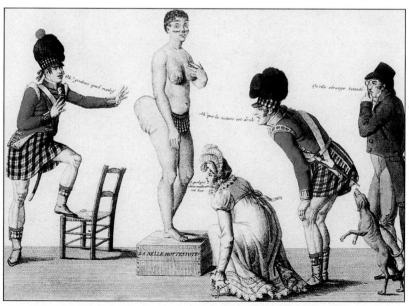

This picture shows the renowned Hottentot woman Sarah Baartman on exhibition in Paris where she was owned and exhibited by an animal trainer. She died in 1815. The artist is satirising the vulgar spectators.

MISS JULIA PASTRANA

Z MEXYKU

WYSTĘPUJĄCA W CYRKU ŚLEZAKA W WARSZAWIE.

Julia in the ring at Warsaw. The man on the right is probably Theodore Lent.

Julia in Moscow, 1859 or 1860. The man on the left presenting her to the fat man is probably Theodore Lent.

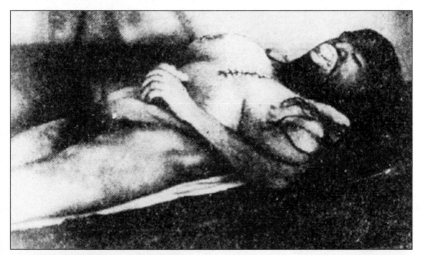

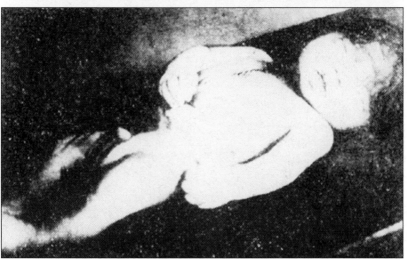

Julia and her son during the embalming process.

This page and opposite: Drawings from the Russian stay in 1859 and 1860.

'The Ape Woman' stuffed, photographed in the early 1860s.
The dress was her own creation,
quite racy by the standards of the time.

'Original mummy. Julia Pastrana and her son':
a German poster from near the end of the nineteenth century.

Marie Bartel was quite swarthy, and could pass as a Mexican. According to the Swedish doctor, Jan Bondeson, her hair and skin syndrome was different from that of Julia Pastrana. This photo dates from the 1870s.

Zenora Pastrana, alias Marie Bartel.

The explorer Carl Lumholtz on his Mexican adventure in Julia Pastrana's homeland. The remarkable dress is a local raincoat.

Lund's Tivoli, Norway's oldest and largest carnival. Luna Park, in Trondheim in 1935, was visited, among others, by King Haakon VII.

Carnival director Haakon Lund in an unusual relaxed moment, in Rena, Norway, 1936. Lund raffled a baby pig, kid or lamb every evening as a prize. The winner was chosen from the numbered entry tickets to the carnival.

Lund's carnival calliope, whose carved figures moved when the music was played.

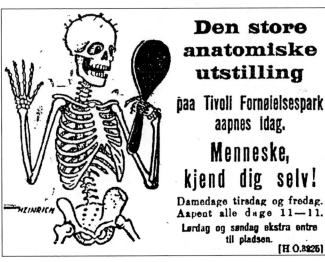

Den store anatomiske utstilling

paa Tivoli Fornøielsespark aapnes idag.

Menneske, kjend dig selv!

Damedage tirsdag og fredag.
Aapent alle dage 11—11.
Lørdag og søndag ekstra entre til pladsen.

[H.O.8825]

'The great anatomical exhibition at Tivoli Amusement Park opens today. Human, know thyself! Ladies' day Tuesday and Friday.'
Advertisement from the Kristiania newspaper *Social-Demokraten*, 1921.

Hermed har jeg Æren at med-
dele det ærede Publikum i Christiania og Omegn, at jeg er ankom-
met og fremviser paa

Tivoli

fra **Søndag den 22de October**
kun en kort Tid, alle Dage
det forhenværende

Hartkopfske
Panoptikon

og anatomiske

Museum,

(det største reisende
Voxkabinet)

indeholder over **1000 Numre,**
Grupper og Figurer, udførte i Vox
i naturlig Størrelse. I intet andet
Voxkabinet forekommer saa mange
berømte Personligheder, hvilket
ogsaa Pressen har fremholdt i de
senere Aar.

Alle existerende Menneskeracer
i sine Nationaldragter.

Berømte Personligheder, kro-
nede Hoveder og Forbrydere, som
Bladene har bragt Underretning
om i de sidste Aar.

!Nyt!
Dreyfus og
Zola.

Bladene har bragt Underretning
om i de sidste Aar.

!Nyt!
Dreyfus og
Zola.

Af Grupperne fremhæves:

De onde Veie

Skildringer af et Liv gjennem
Fristelse og Fald.

7 Grupper, bestaaende af **42**
Figurer. Stor dramatisk og moralsk
Virkning.
Første Gruppe: **Et lykkeligt Hjem
— Fristeren.**
Anden Gruppe: **Faldet — Værtshuset**
Tredje Gruppe: **Forbrydelsen.**
Fjerde Gruppe: **Arrestationen.**
Femte Gruppe: **Konfrontationen
med den myrdedes Lig.**
Sjette Gruppe: **Afskeden i Fængslet.**
Syvende Gruppe: **Paa Skafottet.**

Drypstensgrotten

samt flere plastiske Grupper.

Obs!

Blomsterpiger i Labyrinten

Et Skjønhedsgalleri

af Verdens vakreste Kvinder.
Deriblandt flere prisbelønnet fra
Skjønhedsudstillinger

Findes ikke i noget andet Museum.

En stor anatomisk Afdeling,
hvoriblandt Figurer, som har er-
holdt Medalje paa Verdensudstil-
lingen i Paris, udmærker sig som
fysionomiske Naturfænomener
fremhæves

Juliana Pastrana,

den haarbevoxede Kvinde med
sit Barn.

Abe-, Bjørn-, Hund-, Faar-,
Ugle- og Svin-Mennesker, sammen-
voxede Tvillinger i flere Stadier.

2 Gorillaer,

7 Fod høi, fra Øen Garbo.

Flere af disse Figurer og Præ-
parater er udførte af Artist Daniel,
som er tilkjendt 3 Medailler af
Kunstakademiet i Kjøbenhavn.

Dette Museum er vak-
kert og elegant udstyret
efter Nutidens Fordringer, interes-
sant og lærerigt især for Damer
som Herrer og Børn.

Museet forevises dagligt fra
Kl. 10 Form. til 10 Efterm.

Entré: 35 Øre for Voxne
20 Øre for Børn
under 10 Aar

Advertisement
from *Aftenposten*,
21 October 1899.
Julia, here
incorrectly named
Juliana, is
presented like this
with other freaks:
*Juliana Pastrana,
the hairy Woman
with her Child,
Ape-, Bear-, Dog-,
Sheep-, Owl- and
Pig People,
conjoined Twins
in different
Stages.*

A postcard of Madame Adrienne, sold at carnivals in Germany during the 1940s. The authors suspect that the Hungarian bearded lady was a man in disguise.

Tivolihaven [Tivoli garden] in the centre of Christiania (present-day Oslo),
in the early twentieth century.

Group photograph from 1938: from left to right, 'Gut-Ripper' Magnussen, Arne Andresen ('Arnardo'), and Georg Lerfald.

The Inquisition at work from Lund's Chamber of Horrors.
The picture was taken in Cork, during a tour of Ireland in the summer of 1934.

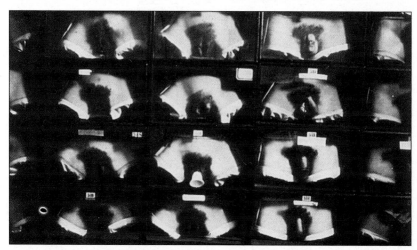

From Lund's 'Hygienic Exhibition', at Elverum Hall, Norway, in 1937. Captions on photos by George Lerfald; the bottom one, showing diseased genitals, may be translated 'The Hygienic Exhibition: sad cases'.

Julia, her son, and the rococo-style carriage. The three collected dust together for more than a hundred years. From an exhibition in Malmö, Sweden, 1970.

The grand Fortuna tent with its painted façade that cost Haakon Lund a small fortune. Sarpsborg, Norway, 1938.

'A dynamic personality with fedora raffishly tilted. . . . The sun-tanned face witnessed a brisk life outdoors at a hundred marketplaces . . . himself the personification of a carnival director with a big C.'
Hans Jæger Lund as described by J. Ødegaard.

NO OTHER WOMAN LOOKED
LIKE HER. FELT LIKE HER.
LOVED LIKE HER...

JOSEPH E.
LEVINE
PRESENTS

the
ape
woman

A CHAMPION CONCORDIA FILM
AN EMBASSY PICTURES RELEASE

La Donna Scimmia was the film's title in its original Italian.
Marco Ferreri was the director, and actor Ugo Tognazzi played a role.

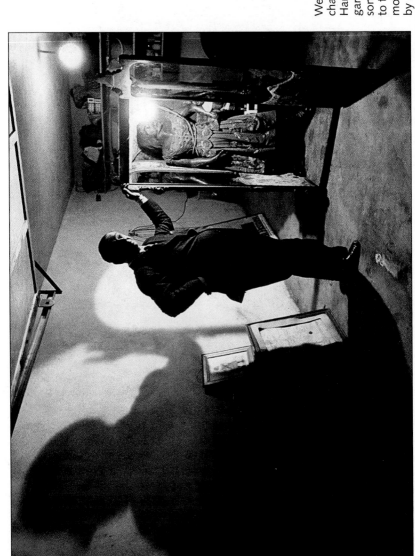

Welcome to the chamber of horrors. . . . Hans Jæger Lund in the garage in 1969. Julia's son can be glimpsed to the right of his mother, who is secured by a sturdy rope.

Emil meets the
bearded lady, lends her
his toy rifle to scare
away the thief,
and saves the day at
Hultfred Plain Market.

Julia & Ruth

There are two stories here, of Julia Pastrana and of Randy and Ruth Rosenson who manage the attraction for Lund's Tivoli of Norway. The monkey-faced Mexican was born in 1832 and died in Russia in 1860, while touring as an attraction. The embalmed body was brought over this year to appear with Gooding's Million-Dollar Midways. Says Ruth: "He was checking out $50 worth of groceries in Florida and I was in line behind him, and I saw all those Green Stamps." She followed him to the parking lot to see if he was saving them, "and we stuck together." He also has a Kennedy Wax Museum.

(AB)

This 1972 photograph shows Julia in the background, with the show business couple Ruth and Randy Rosenson, who helped Lund with the US exhibition.

On tour in the USA Hans Jæger Lund
standing before the specially built exhibition trailer.

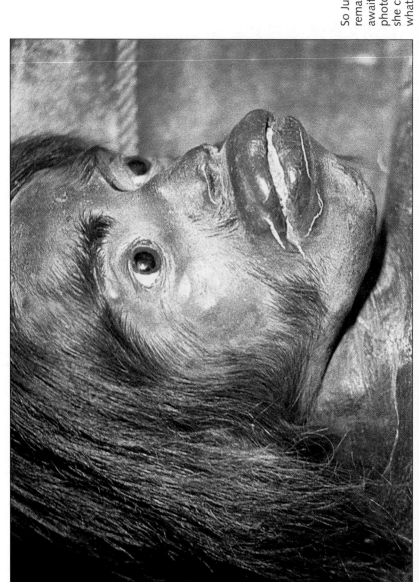

So Julia Pastrana remains in storage, awaiting her fate, as photographed here. If she could speak to us, what would she say?

by a Scandinavian showman named Andersen, and Julia and son changed hands yet again. We know little of what happened over the next twenty years, but she was clearly trundled about all over Europe under a succession of new owners. Eventually she was sold to a German freak museum and chamber of horrors – perhaps the very one that had hired her from Lent decades before. There she remained for a long time, slowly descending into obscurity. She was no longer news, a sensation or a 'femme à barbe', no longer a nondescript or an 'interessante frau' – now she was merely a dust-collecting mummy. Was her long journey finally over?

Meanwhile, on the other side of the world, in that same Mexican landscape that Julia had left forty years before, something important was happening. As the ape-woman was being forgotten by those who had seen her alive, her own people were being discovered and described for the very first time. The Norwegian explorer and ethnographer Carl Lumholtz, who spent five years during the 1890s in the wilds of western Mexico, wrote:

> As a well-bred dog or horse may show finer and nobler traits than many a man, so it seems to me, after my long experience with the Mexican Indians, that in their natural state they are in certain points superior, not only to the average Mexican half-caste, but to the common run of whites. We are brought up to look upon primitive peoples as synonyms of all that is crude, evil, and vicious. Nothing could be more erroneous.[8]

Lumholtz was a curious, adventurous man who had travelled for years in the least known areas of Australia and Borneo. He wrote a number of travel accounts, including *Unknown Mexico: A record of five years' exploration among the tribes of the Sierra Madre*, published in 1902. This is the first scientific work concerning the area and is still, a hundred years later, considered a major source. Lumholtz's interest was first captured by the unusual cave dwellings of the American south-west, where extinct tribes had lived (echoing the supposed cave life of Julia Pastrana and her mother). Lumholtz wanted to find the survivors of the cliff-dwellers. A major expedition was prepared, financed by large scientific societies in North America. Both the American government and Porfirio Diaz, president of Mexico, supported Lumholtz, and he obtained permission to roam freely around Mexico's most inaccessible areas.

The expedition recorded plant and animal life, carried out archaeological excavations, and undertook anthropological research among the Mexican Indians. Lumholtz met the Tarahumara, the Tepehuán, the Cora, the Huichol, the Tepe-cano and several other native groups. He wrote: 'Of most of these tribes little more than their names were known, and I have brought back large collections illustrating their ethnical and anthropological status, besides extensive information in regard to their customs, religion, traditions, and myths.'[9] What distinguished Lumholtz was his sober and positive description of the Indian tribes. To view them as anything other than inferior and backward was unusual at a time when the idea of white racial superiority was spreading, and western man was seen as the rightful ruler of the world.

Lumholtz had an open-minded respect for the natives, and came to know them well. He wrote about their gods and demons, their relations with the bearded Mexicans – whom they detested – and their thoughts about other Indian tribes and customs. He did not refer unscientifically to the 'Root Digger Indians', but did mention several groups of primitive natives, including the mysterious Cocoyomes, who Lumholtz heard of from the Tarahumara.

The Tarahumara, who inhabited the large forests of Sinoloa where Julia spent her first years, described the Cocoyomes to Lumholtz:

They were the first people in the world, were short in stature, and did not eat corn. They subsisted mainly on herbs. They were also cannibals devouring each other as well as the Tarahumares. The Cocoyomes lived in caves on the high cliffs of the sierra, and in the afternoon came down, like deer, to drink in the rivers . . . Long ago, when the Cocoyomes were very bad, the sun came down to the earth and burned nearly all of them; only a few escaped into the big caves.[10]

In other words they were short, mainly vegetarian, primitive, and lived in caves. Although much suggested the Cocoyomes were purely mythical, their description was very similar to that of Julia's apparent tribal beginnings. In any case, for the first time the area of her birth was being made familiar through books published in Mexico, the United States and England, not to mention the cold and distant northern land that would be her final earthly destination. A few years before Julia's mummy and that of her child came to Oslo, Lumholtz wrote, regarding his Mexican travels:

There was. . . . no other sign that [these caves] had ever been inhabited. . . . Indeed, on first sight there was nothing in the cave to indicate that they had ever been used by man; but below the dust we came upon a hard, concrete floor, and after digging through this . . . we fortunately struck a skull, and then came upon the body of a man. After this we disinterred that of a mother, holding a child in her arms . . . All were in a marvellous state of preservation . . . this imparted to the dead a mummy-like appearance, but there was nothing to suggest that embalming or other artificial means of preservation of the bodies had been used.[11]

Were these exhumed corpses distant relatives of Julia Pastrana? A mother and child together in death, shoulder to shoulder while the years go by, like Julia and her son? 'All Indians believe in a life after death,' Lumholtz had written. But Julia's relatives in Mexico would have found it difficult to comprehend her own remarkable afterlife, a journey not yet over even then.

6

A Cultural and Historical Treasure

The First World War was over and Norway – small and neutral – had escaped lightly. Despite the sinking of a few freighters, the war had created an economic boom for the Norwegians. But a postwar slump had spread rapidly into Scandinavia and even though they were on the fringes of war-torn Europe, the Norwegians were struggling. Banks and industrial companies were going bankrupt, and tens of thousands of workers were being fired each year. The Norwegian labour movement was big, militant and unusually aggressive, threatening revolution, as did the country's Moscow-oriented communists. The bourgeoisie feared for their lives, and there were constant governmental crises, with parliamentary quarrels about the church, prohibition and the national language. The country's capital Kristiania (re-named Oslo four years later)[1] was an unsettled place. People were unsure of the future. They wanted to be entertained. And who better to provide it than the legendary Haakon Lund:

> He stood before the gate wearing an enormous hat, a Kaiser Wilhelm moustache, and a thick coat. . . . He was a carnival man of the grand type. Hard, clever, ruthless when necessary, and nice when it suited him. He originally came from northern Norway and had done a bit of this, a bit of that, before he started with carnivals. Not even

the tailor-made coat could hide his powerful muscles, built up when he was a navvy on the Bergen rail line. During winter, he travelled back to his house in Berlin, returning from there in the spring in ample time before each new season.

He could easily have with him then a whole railway train full of equipment, which threw him into innumerable conflicts with the customs authorities.[2]

That was him, Haakon Lund, Norway's carnival king number one. He was a big figure on the European scene just after the end of the First World War; he owned and ran the travelling show Lund's Tivoli, also known as Luna Park, that toured all over Scandinavia, while his wife owned the Indra Park amusement arcade in Berlin. In Kristiania, Lund ran *Den Kulørte By* (The Gaudy City), an entertainment centre on the city's west side. Luna Park was a giant enterprise that took two weeks to set up at each new venue. The big top was 106ft long by 23ft wide, and there were a dozen other smaller but still impressive tents. All were surrounded by large wooden shutters, supported on solid metal frames.

Lund had ambitions, and visited only the larger cities and towns. He was a smart, hard-driving businessman, who had started empty-handed and wound up with seventy railway cars full of valuable carnival equipment. He was a colourful and exciting personality, like so many of his fellow showmen – show business demanded a lot of energy, and Lund had plenty to give. His strongest card was an instinct for a good show, for knowing what the people wanted. He also knew how important it was to have breadth and variety in the acts, especially during the high season of spring and summer, and also during autumn and winter when the big show was unable to tour. That's when it was smart to have extra tricks up your sleeve, and it was that belief which prompted him to buy a cabinet of curiosities in Berlin offered to him by an American showman with money problems.

Quite a collection landed in Lund's lap – thousands of objects of all kinds. There were quantities of human body parts preserved in great glass jars filled with spirit. There were monstrously malformed heads, and deformed embryos of Siamese twins; an entire human skin nailed to a plank with its scalp intact on top; unborn children with scales instead of skin, with only one eye in the middle of the forehead; and specimens of loathsome and grotesque diseases. There were also stuffed and preserved animals, two-headed calves, beings with human bodies and fishes' tails and much, much more.

Lund also landed a wax museum. It had been originally made for medical instruction and showed the extreme effects of venereal diseases in full bloom and living colour. Totally unappetising, of course, but good business – a mix of the titillating and frightening, a superb combination. And then right at the back of one of the storage trailers he found a large glass coffin hidden behind a fringed drape. Lund rubbed his hands together. He could smell money.

MIDGETS ARE NOT STRONG

In 1926, German radio broadcast a lecture on carnival and travelling show business, delivered by the circus historian Alfred Lehmann. He used much of his time to reminisce about the well-known personality in the German entertainment world, Julia Pastrana, who many listeners would no doubt remember. Her tragic fate deserved re-telling. Finally, he asked if any listeners knew where the mummified body of Julia Pastrana could be found. Many listeners replied, all with a story about seeing her mummified corpse. Some remembered a certain Zenora Pastrana – was it the same person? But none gave him a direct answer. The man who did know the answer was a carnival king from Norway and Lund rarely had the time to listen to the radio. In the summer he was on tour with Lund's Tivoli, and in the winter there was the amusement park in Berlin. And now there was the Hygienic and Anatomical Exhibition to run in Norway. For this was the name under which his newly purchased cabinet of curiosities toured up and down the country, thrilling and chilling Norwegian audiences. There was the woman sought by German radio, somewhere in an old circus trailer in icy Norway. Silent, dusty, with a child at her side, but not without a certain dignity.

She was described in an extensive advertisement in a Norwegian newspaper of 1921:

In her time, the dancer performed in the European big cities and died giving birth in Moscow. She was half-human, half-animal, one of those remarkable creations that gives the impression that when she was born, Nature could not decide what it really wanted to make. You'll chill when you see her face, and ask yourself involuntarily if it is a human one, or an ape's or even whether Nature decided to remind humanity every few years about its ancestors, so that in spite of all the veneer of civilisation's tinsel, mankind will be reminded of where it comes from. In that manner, Julia Pastrana, even as a mummy, with her delicate and supple body upon which sits the head of an ape, raises the serious and nagging question: What is human?[3]

Similar questions had probably been asked on earlier occasions, since Julia wasn't exactly new to Norway. Her name had appeared in newspaper advertisements for foreign freak shows and wax displays touring the country in the 1890s. In 1894 she could have been seen, with wax figures of royals and murderers, at the Colosseum Panoptikon in the capital. From October 1899 until April 1900 she could be seen at the Hartkopfian Panopticon and Anatomical Museum[4] at Tivoli. And in 1889 the Norwegian magazine *Folkebladet* ran an article about Zenora Pastrana. But, luckily for Lund, few remembered her in the 1920s. It was time for Julia to make a comeback.

A Russian carriage was part of the deal when Lund bought Julia's remains in 1921. This elaborate object, ostentatiously decorated with velvet, silk ribbons and ruching, would have stood out like some fancy theatre prop for most sturdy small-town Norwegians. The more thoughtful may have seen it as a symbol of past glory, with its stuffed mummy standing in the shadows. There was a touch of decay about both the mummy and the carriage, and the small doll-like shape perched at the side. It could all be seen as a picture of the collapse of old Russia, now supplanted by the new Soviet Union.

A genuine Russian document was also displayed. It carried Sokolov's signature, and was accompanied by a German translation, stamped and countersigned by a Dresden notary, the year 1864 clearly visible at the bottom.[5] The showmen informed visitors that it was the original certificate for the stuffing of mummies, translated and approved by the German authorities just four years after the deaths of the woman and child. The Norwegian countryfolk scratched their heads. A certificate for getting stuffed! The embalming, which included the mounting of glass eyes, was said to have cost 5,350 roubles, a small fortune in those days. According to the document, the glass eyes were the only parts of Julia that were not genuine.[6]

Even though no certificates are needed for membership in the world of the freak show, nevertheless there were internal, unwritten laws, its own code, as it were, that regulated relations between insiders and outsiders. Members of the carnival and freak show subculture were always looked down upon by proper society. As a result, they felt tighter bonds with those of their own kind. These are things that ordinary, stick-in-the-mud citizens – 'suckers' in the subculture's derogatory term – neither could, nor would understand. Nor were such things any of their business. This is important to point out, since show people's daily bread was dependent on surprise and mystery. You didn't discuss things too much with ordinary punters, and you never revealed the tricks of the trade. These often involved deceit, swindling and deception, or, at best, great exaggeration and misleading claims. This has always been part of the game; the easily-suckered idiots of the world always want to be fooled. With regard to that, a true showman will never show remorse. On the contrary, it is a matter of pride to have hoodwinked spectators in the most elegant and refined fashion.

On the other hand, you never cheat your own local colleagues. A rich sideshow owner far away on the other side of the country, like Barnum and the Cardiff Giant – okay. But never those you work with, especially not within the world of the real outcasts, the inner circles of the freak show. Awful consequences can result. The earliest exposition of this was given in Tod Browning's spectacular film *Freaks*, from 1932. Seldom, or perhaps never, have such unusual actors been used in a Hollywood production. Even if the 1930s American public expected something out of the ordinary from the director of *Dracula*, no one could have foreseen this.

'With a cast of real rarities, this is a sensitive, powerful masterpiece of the horror genre,' wrote one critic years later. The film's marketing made it clearer still in the original film poster: 'For pure sensationalism, *Freaks* tops any picture yet produced. It's more fantastic and grotesque than any shocker ever written.'[7] The film deals with a travelling sideshow, and most of the actors were real freaks, malformed and handicapped people of all types, many of them known contemporary figures, playing themselves.

Here were Siamese twins, the famous Hilton Sisters; a 'half boy' missing the lower part of his body, who walked with his hands; the almost as famous Johnny Eck; several so-called 'pinheads' (small, retarded people with a characteristically pointed head shape); and a black man – a 'human torso' – without arms or legs, who rolled cigarettes with his mouth. There was a young woman – a so-called 'armless wonder'– who ate with her feet, and some dwarfs. One of these was Angelo Rossitto, twenty-four at the time and already an experienced actor, who would, fifty-three years later, play his last on-screen role with Mel Gibson in the Mad Max film *Beyond the Thunderdome*. During his sixty-year-long career he played in more than forty feature films, without ever getting rich or famous. In order to survive, he always needed to run a newspaper stand on the side. While *Freaks* was being filmed, he was in any case among his own kind, those who are different.

There was also a bearded lady, the renowned artiste Lady Olga. She had the longest beard known to be possessed by a woman – fourteen inches. Lady Olga was no well-adjusted woman in ordinary life. Known to over-indulge in drink, she was testy and violent while intoxicated. Her real name was Jane Barnell; she started in the business when only four years old. She was known as Princess Olga early in her career, but the title was modified to 'Lady' once she became older and less charming. At one point, an imaginative manager suggested she colour her beard blue, in order to appear as Lady Bluebeard. She rejected the suggestion, and later left the circus in protest after her colleagues went on strike. Strongly conservative, she wanted nothing to do with striking socialists. She was one of those who later strongly attacked *Freaks*, claiming that the actors had no idea of what they were getting into. That might certainly have been the case. Some of them only had the mental capacity of small children – for which group, by the way, the film was not suitable. 'Children will not be permitted to see this picture! Adults not in normal health are urged not to!' as the film advertisements warned.[8]

Central to the plot is the dwarf Hans, who falls in love with the beautiful but evil trapeze artist Cleopatra. She is a woman of normal stature, very attractive, and calculating right down to the bone. She at first sees the romance as a ludicrous joke. She is already attached to the strong man of the show, Hercules, who is as morally challenged as she is herself. Everything changes when she finds out about the fortune Hans has just inherited. He suddenly becomes more interesting, and Cleopatra and Hercules conspire to get hold of the money.

'Midgets are not strong,' she tells her big lover.[9] 'He could get sick. . . . It could be done,' she adds meaningfully. She begins an affair with the naïve Hans, and soon they decide to marry. During the wedding banquet, all the artists sitting around the table sing their special song, where the refrain runs 'One of us! One of us!' This is to demonstrate that Cleopatra is on the way to joining the freak show fellowship. She, however, doesn't want it. Both she and the giant Hercules, who is also there and makes open passes at the bride, detest the small and mis-shapen people. They show this clearly, by humiliating Hans in front of all his friends and by lashing out at the others for good measure.

They later attempt to poison the bridegroom to obtain the fortune, but this is discovered by the others. The film culminates in a gruesome chase between the carnival trailers on a dark and rainy night. Hercules is stabbed to death by several of the malformed acting together. Cleopatra is so cut up and mutilated as to be unrecognisable. At the beginning of the film, without being told who she is, the viewer catches a glimpse of her after this treatment – without legs, with scarred face, clad in a feathered costume as some grotesque 'chicken woman'. She can only cackle and blather, ruined for life, mentally disturbed as she is. After this, the film rolls forward, and only at its end do we understand who the unfortunate woman was. Cleopatra has really become 'One of us!', as the others put it.

The most memorable scene in *Freaks* is when the raging artists creep and crawl towards their victim, with or without legs and arms, through mud and rain, with murder in their eyes and knives clenched in their teeth. This display of savagery and hatred by the freaks is the part of the film that has been most heavily criticised, both then and later.

The film was not a financial success: it was too frightening, and too unsavoury. It was immediately banned in Great Britain. On economic grounds, MGM quickly removed it from the market. Thirty years went by before it could be seen again, this time for specially interested aficionados of the camp film genre. Wounded, Tod Browning withdrew from the film business, and never went to the movies again.

But the negative contemporary reactions had nothing to do with the freak show as such. There were still many such attractions around in the thirties and later, both in Europe and the United States. One of the best-known was Percilla Bejano, the Monkey Girl. Originally from Puerto Rico, she was reminiscent of Julia Pastrana, with a hairy body, a broad nose, and a thick full beard. In contrast to her predecessor, she had a long and happy life together with her husband Emmet Bejano, the Alligator-Skinned Man. He suffered from a special disease that turned his epidermis into a sort of scaly surface, giving it the appearance of reptile's skin. Together, they made up the 'World's Strangest Married

Couple', who toured the United States during the thirties and following decades. They retired in 1985. Percilla lived a long time, not dying until autumn 2000, in the small town of Gibsonton, Florida. Gibsonton has in fact become a special refuge, a place to where show people and freak show stars can retire in their later years. Here live giants and dwarfs, fat men and ape women.

Hairiness, it must be said, is not exclusive to women. Another early twentieth-century freak show star was the Russian Stephan Bilgraski, born in 1880 and known as Lionel, the Lion-Faced Boy. He had hair of up to 30 centimetres length over large parts of his body and on his face: on the nose right up to the eyes, and on his brow. His mother while pregnant supposedly saw her husband torn to pieces by lions – at least according to P.T. Barnum, who nonchalantly overlooked the absence of the king of beasts from Russian fauna. Lionel toured both sides of the Atlantic all his life, and attained special renown in France as *l'Homme Léon*, the lion man.

The level of interest was generally high for freaks and hairy individuals of all sorts. In Germany, the elegant Madame Adrienne, a Hungarian performer and 'moustache lady' of dubious sexual identity, had great success in the 1930s and '40s with her full beard and dress. Travelling shows were one of the most popular forms of entertainment all over Europe, and the exhibition of deformed people only made things even more exotic. Similar amusements were also found in the far north of the continent.

. . . WITH THE HEAD OF AN APE AND COVERED WITH HAIR

'Furthermore, we have puppet theatres, Laterna Magica, mechanical wax cabinets, magicians, giants and giantesses, albinos or girls allergic to light, Siamese twins, strongmen, fire swallowers, snakemen and India rubber ladies, midget oxen, *giant* oxen, and odd animals of all sorts'. So wrote Rudolf Muus in his book about Oslo life in the good old days.[10] Norway's capital has a long tradition of light entertainment. Admittedly, the custom of large public carnivals and masquerades disappeared in the seventeenth century, but it continued on a smaller scale. The festivities had to be decorous and supervised by the authorities. In the mid-nineteenth century, there was a popular market place at Ruseløkken, above the shabby Vika district west of Oslo's harbour. Fireworks were let off from here, and there was drinking and loud celebration, to the shock and disgust of law-abiding burghers. Social classes did not mix, either while amusing themselves, or while following other pursuits.

Around the middle of the century jugglers and sleight-of-hand artists came in with a vengeance. Tightrope walkers, sword swallowers, clowns, wild animal tamers and strongmen made their entry into Norway. They were allowed to perform more or less freely in the Pipervika and Christiania Markets of Oslo, or wherever else they turned up. The public took to this enthusiastically, and new troupes – many from Italy and Russia – offered unknown and incredible spectacles. At Christiania market at Youngstorvet a living mermaid was the sensation one summer. She had been captured in a net in the Atlantic, and lay upon the exhibition table smiling enticingly. 'The people stood around dumbfounded at this living marvel', as a contemporary source put it.[11] One spectator was sceptical, and tore her tail off. It was made of tin, and the mermaid ran off on a pair of shapely legs. The public was furious, and the police closed the show.

After a while, the demand for popular entertainment became so great that a purpose-built, permanent circus building was erected in 1895. It held 2,500 people, and stood at the entertainment centre called Tivoli Amusement Park in the centre of town, not far from the Norwegian Parliament. For over two centuries, the place had been a centre for popular entertainments in more or less respectable forms. The district of Vika was close by, with its bordellos and sleazy watering holes. As far as possible, a respectable image was presented, since the Tivoli Gardens were intended for the broadest spectrum of the populace. In principle, both rich and poor could mingle here, as long as they could pay their way. There was an attractive garden to stroll in, a pleasant café for refreshments, a shooting gallery, and variety acts in the circus tent. On occasion, travelling shows would rent smaller locations where they could display their exotic sights with remarkable artists.

The old carnival man Fredrik W. Ilboe described one of these performances:

He advertised with big posters such sensations as 'The Full-Bearded Woman', 'The Limbless Female' or 'The Talking Head'. The latter sat on a large round tub, daubed with flecks of blood, and in the weak light of paraffin lamps, was very unsettling when it opened its eyes, moving its lips, and told in short, breathy sentences about love, jealousy, drama, and death. Adults 25 øre, children 10 øre.[12]

There were also travelling circuses, that actively advertised their arrival in the city. The Leonard Hancke Circus printed colourful posters when it came to Kristiania in the late nineteenth century, with the words:

The only Circus in Scandinavia that provides its own electric Lighting with its own Motor and Dynamo, transported in a wagon constructed especially for that purpose. Austrian Wind and String Orchestra of 10 men.

Evening gala on last day. Please note: The Director will give away 12 of his large Photographs which are on display at Olsen's Bookstore.[13]

One of the most fascinating things that could be experienced was the travelling wax cabinet, with famous historical characters, and a terrifying selection of horrors. Frèdrik W. Ilboe remembered it:

Even more thrills were had when the wax cabinet came. Just the sight of the wax-pale, deathly yellow full-sized figures of the Emperor Napoleon, Bismarck, Queen Victoria, or a quite real Chinese, was a bit frightening. But above all the rest, was – as it said in the advertisement – 'Gruesome scenes from the Inquisition! Torture chamber, Naked Young Witches, the Spanish Cape,[14] with much, much more. Adults 50 øre. Discount for school classes accompanied by teachers.'[15]

Haakon Lund owned just such a cabinet – possibly the same one visited by Ilboe – with Napoleon, Bismarck, and many other celebrities and a chamber of horrors too, with scenes of torture, naked witches and the whole works. It was a popular feature that was constantly being renewed. Later on, Churchill and Hitler received their places in the collection. It was important to keep up with the times, and to offer the public a broad spectrum of entertainment. Therefore, Lund kept not just one wax cabinet, but two.

As already mentioned, he had found the other one – of a more bizarre character – in Germany. It had preserved embryos, wax depictions of human illnesses and last if not least, Julia Pastrana and her son. It was without question Norway's most remarkable and repulsive private collection, but it did at the same time have a certain medical value.

The collection filled a large part of a storage hall of 300 square metres, and comprised more than 8,000 objects, stacked four to five metres high. Out on the road, many trailers were needed to move it around. Lund was an active person, and did not rest on his laurels. In the 1920s, he had become very well-to-do, and not just because of the carnival and entertainment activity. His trading in jewellery, gold and diamonds was just as important. The carnival king even dealt in antiques, through his own shop in the centre of Oslo. When it came to Julia Pastrana, he wanted to display her in more elevated surroundings than had hitherto been the case.

The wax cabinet with Julia was now presented as a medical chamber of monstrosities, since it required emphatic marketing. Lund did not want simply to create a sensation. The exhibition had an element of popular education about it, and in addition to its rather inappropriate name of the Hygienic and Anatomical Exhibition, it carried a slogan, 'Humanity, Know Thyself'. Each object was accompanied by a large poster, with more or less correct historical and biological information. Julia's life was also outlined, in unclear, exaggerated ways, and the original embalming document was also included, so that people could make up their own minds. But it wasn't history or medical science that drew people to the show, even though Lund had hired medical students as guides and demonstrators. They went around in white lab coats describing the various deformities and venereal diseases to their appalled audience.

One of them was a failed former medical student called Magnussen, popularly known as *Bukspretter'n* (the Gut-Ripper), who struggled with a serious drinking problem. Before being thrown out of university he had picked up a smattering of Latin which sounded quite impressive to visitors. But the unreliable Magnussen was away one day and Lund noticed a terrible smell coming from the chamber of horrors. The reason was soon obvious: the deformed Siamese twins who should have been floating in spirits were now immersed in water. Magnussen the drunken ne'er-do-well had taken the alcohol and replaced it with water. Lund could imagine the rest. Magnussen was dragged semi-conscious from his home and promptly driven direct to hospital to have his stomach pumped. Later, more dead than alive, he went off to see Lund, was roundly cursed and immediately fired.

The twins were saved, everything returned to normal and the wax figures continued to provide chills and thrills. 'And I don't mind,' Lund said, 'if the remaining guides want to lay it on a bit thick', which they did. Some of the wax figures had built-in drawers in their bodies which could be pulled out one by one, to reveal inner decay and syphilitic rottenness. The students added plenty of graphic detail. Quite regularly, spectators would be overcome by nausea, and have to make a bolt for the door. And one cold winter day, at the small town of Årnes, a few miles north-east of Oslo, a hefty lumberjack fainted during an intimate exposition on anatomy. He crashed into a large, hot wood stove and four men had to carry him out. Having escaped without injury, his embarrassed excuse was: 'But it was all those awful intestines . . .'. Which of course amounted to excellent free publicity. People told their friends and acquaintances about their gruesome experiences and the news spread.

Julia's travels took her all over Norway, and by the end of the twenties she was appearing in big fairs in Bergen and Trondheim. But much of the time Julia was shown in the cities and towns of south-east Norway, with or without the waxworks cabinet. Sometimes she drew the crowds, especially in the smaller places, but not always. In the thirties, she was once on display in the small sleepy town of

Gjøvik, in a shop in the Grand Hotel, and no one paid any attention at all.

Occasionally Lund would select the choicest items from his two cabinets of curiosities, and send a small collection on the road. In the years between the wars, the carnival worker Georg Lerfald was assigned to several of these tours. His job was to keep the collection in order, give talks to the public and keep Julia presentable. In his wide-ranging memoirs, written many years later, he was unable to remember all the details of her background and history. But he couldn't forget Julia.

> I recall very well how she looked, something I won't forget – not after dusting her off and tidying her up lots of times! She was hairy over her entire body and face, too, which was awfully like an ape's. The hands and feet were like those of other humans, and her height, I believe, was 1.42 metres. She was supposed to have been a very skilled dancer, and could walk the tightrope. She had a child by her impresario, but it didn't survive. She has appeared on most of the big stages and circuses throughout Europe.[16]

Georg also doubled as the crocodile keeper for several seasons when they kept four aggressive beasts in a small pool. In addition he was responsible for four frisky monkeys, which, to his constant consternation, escaped whenever they got the chance, leading the police on massive chases through Oslo's parks. But the crocs were the worst and, one winter night in Østlandet, there was a discharge of electric current into the pool. The reptiles were nearly boiled while Lerfald toiled like a madman to save them and himself. He was successful, but looking after Julia and the wax figures was by far the preferred option.

Lerfeld recalled the exhibition in great detail:

First the historical part: Napoleon at St Helena, Dreyfus on Devil's Island, martyrs on the rack, the Muscle Man and Dante's Inferno. The tortures of the damned had the sturdy Trondheimers fainting left and right. The natural history section contained the Anatomical Venus, a well-formed female figure in 48 parts where you worked your way inward while you removed layer after layer, first the skin, then the muscles, thereafter into the chest and abdominal cavities until you reached the most secret and innermost organs. Julia Pastrana sat in her glass cabinet, with her monkey face, covered with hair from her head to her toes.'[17]

On one occasion, at the small mining city of Kongsberg, where the carnival had been nine days, a large delegation from the local hospital came visiting. Lerfald was told to show them around 'the wax'. He dreaded pretending to be medically knowledgeable before twenty doctors and nurses, but all went well. The doctors were especially impressed by the Anatomical Venus, but even more by the collection's genuine anatomical sensation:

> The doctors were very interested in Julia Pastrana's 'mummy'. I told them what I knew about the embalmed ape-woman, and pointed out besides the information on the 'mummy' and the embalming certificate which was displayed in Julia's carrying case.[18]

The only problem was that Julia was now getting quite moth-eaten, and the silk dress was no longer very elegant. She still looked life-like in the shadows of the carriage but her fame and likewise her shock effect began to diminish. In 1940 Lund rented the Håndverkeren restaurant in Oslo, and set up his chamber of horrors inside, once more under the banner 'Humanity, Know Thyself'. His other wax cabinet,

Castan's Panoptikon, was also there. Neither Napoleon nor the Inquisition in wax, nor even Julia Pastrana in her glass cage aroused much interest. The unmentionables preserved in spirits, the cut-off heads and herpes in wax were what shocked. People keeled over, dropping like flies.

In autumn 1943, a remarkable turn occurred in Julia's existence. The German occupation authorities had her under scrutiny as part of the big exhibition at Håndverkeren, and now it looked as if time was up for her and the wax cabinet. There was another mood in entertainment now, and attitudes towards freak shows were changing. In the nineteenth century the public was often impressed and fascinated by what they saw on stage, whether that was singing ape-women, or other remarkable people. Most people then had not travelled abroad or read about natural wonders, and were an audience ripe for what travelling shows had on offer. Even scientists didn't have much of value to say when they pontificated about freaks. The deformed people on stage were always 'unique' and 'fantastic', and the public was easily fooled.

Around the turn of the century, a change occurred. Science had become more sober and trustworthy, and most understood that freaks were sick, people with developmental defects. Those previous advantages, those things that made the performers mysterious, were now seen as infirmities and little else. The public still came to gawk, but their attitude was different, perhaps less respectful and more cynical. Simultaneously, many felt uneasy at seeing the mentally backward on stage. Humane factors played a role, but other, more brutal factors were involved. The mentally retarded were simply aesthetically unpleasant, and more and more spectators questioned the right to existence of such individuals. Doctrines about racial purity and hygiene were spreading throughout the western world, and the strong and perfect human was soon a common ideal. This hostility reached a peak when the Second World War broke out, and there was less room for those who were different. Both those alive, and those dead.

In May 1943, the 34-year-old Georg Wilhelm Müller came to Norway. He wanted to make his mark, and as a high-ranking Nazi he had great power. Already in 1936, he had been adjutant for Goebbels himself. In 1940 he was sent to Norway, and the Western Front the year after, where he was wounded. In 1943 he was returning to Norway as chief of the *Hauptabteilung Volksaufklärung und Propaganda*, the Nazi mass propaganda machine.

He was also responsible for the control of radio, books and newspapers, and other cultural activities. As a key member of the SS, with the title *Ministerialdirigent* (Ministerial Assistant Director) for Norway, he was seen as the most unpleasant individual in the ruling German administration. He was an expert at staying in favour with Goebbels in Germany and *Reichscommissar* Terboven in Norway.[19]

Initially, Lund's displays were a matter for lower ranking officers, not Müller himself.[20] In Nazi eyes it was a degenerate, morally reprehensible exhibition, and Lund was told all the wax displays and biological material were to be considered as confiscated, to be handed over immediately. All the wax would be melted down for the benefit of the German state, to be used for candles. Lund had never heard such nonsense, but had to tread carefully. Even though the Nazis possessed overwhelming power, Lund was not the kind to give up easily. Travelling circus and carnival people were outcasts in Nazi Germany, especially as many came from eastern and southern Europe, and were not exactly Germanic. As travelling people, they were like gypsies and tinkers, types that should be kept apart from good Aryans. Even worse, some freak show employees were handicapped or dwarfs.

In Gunther Grass's novel *The Tin Drum*, the main character Oskar, who stopped growing while still a child, visits a circus touring Nazi Germany. A dwarf at the circus, Herr Bebra, suggests that Oskar joins them. 'I'd rather be in the audience,' replies Oskar.[21] Herr Bebra becomes serious, and explains that '[You] and I don't belong among the watchers. We've got to stand on stage, in front of the arena. We've got to be the play-actors, and steer the action, or else the others will decide for us. And they mean us no good! . . . They're coming! They're filling the rally grounds! They're holding torch-lit parades! They're filling the stands, and preaching our destruction from there.' In other words, confront the challenge before it is too late. The two characters later meet again under different circumstances; Bebra is now employed to entertain Nazi officers. It's a matter of survival: the alternative doesn't bear thinking about.

Lund's situation was nowhere near as bad as that. He had business dealings in Germany years before the Nazis took over, and was not about to give up without a fight. But the German authorities had already created great problems for his family. In 1939 his wife had received a clear demand from the Nazis that she must be permanently resident in Germany by the end of the year. Her carnival in Berlin had to run from Germany alone, not from Norway, otherwise it would be confiscated for the benefit of the state. But the Lunds never moved back to Germany and there was no warmth in Lund's feelings for the Nazis.

However, Lund needed to get on with the regime in Norway. Otherwise, he would see all his operations there closed down. Everything would be lost, and hundreds of employees would be out of work. He had invested large sums in his exhibitions. Melt them down? Bollocks! Lund began discussions with the authorities, and proposed that he should be allowed to keep the collection. In return he would hand a part of his income over to the state as a special tax. If the displays were too much for Norwegian stomachs, they could be taken over the border to tour Sweden. The big man with the Kaiser Wilhelm moustache knew the art of persuasion and, in the end, even *Ministerialdirigent* Müller agreed. The money was one thing; more important to the authorities was the removal of such morally objectionable material from the roads of Norway. As soon as possible. Since Lund was already living in Sweden by then, and had interests in the Liseburg Tivoli in Gothenburg, obeying the order cost him almost nothing. And it wasn't likely that the Nazis would receive any money from him – carnival kings didn't hand over money easily.

NO OTHER WOMAN . . . LOVED LIKE HER

Lund was not an easy man to deal with, for the Nazis or anyone else. He was especially difficult and strict with his son, Hans Jæger Lund. Lund employed him from early on as a helper, and 'ensured that junior got the longest hours – and the least pay', as one carnival worker said. Hans started working for his father when he was nine years old but it was not what he wanted to do. The boy had grown up on his grandparents' farm and really wanted to be a farmer, but his father had his own way. Carnival was the way to go.

When he was aged seventeen Hans rebelled and enrolled at the agricultural college at Toten, not far from Hamar. Nonetheless, the year after, he was back with his father travelling around the country for a couple of seasons. His father drove him harder than before and it ended with the incensed Hans leaving the family business. He tried lorry-driving but discovered that the carnival was in his blood. Soon after, Hans was back in the business as the co-owner of a smaller carnival at Sagene in Oslo. The next year he bought his own tent, set up a shooting gallery and went into business for himself with four air rifles. But it didn't go well. Hans had to sleep in the leaky tent all summer and winter. Later he recalled how he had to get up early, shivering in the cold, and run barefoot in the snow to try and get himself warm. After that he made things up with his father, and learnt much about running a business properly.

In 1951 his mother, Charlotta, died. Until the very end she had helped her husband and now the old carnival director had to run things alone. Her death was a hard blow but he didn't let that stop him, and organised a stylish funeral. In keeping with the Lund family's colourful traditions, a wake was arranged in Gothenburg where the elderly couple had lived for a long time. Carnival people gathered from near and far, including the family's employee for many years, Georg Lerfald.

The events made an indelible impression on him, and he described the funeral many years later in his memoirs:

> Wake in St Erik's Cellar, where the funeral party arrived at 1700 hours. The table was decked with various dishes, and also beer and aquavit . . . The priest made a speech about Haakon Lund, on this day of great sorrow, and then ended the eulogy by proposing a toast for the grieving husband! It can't be denied that he bumbled a few words near the end. And with the coffee spiked, he was legless. I never saw such a drunken priest! Fortunately, he disappeared rather early, helped out by the head waiter. Afterwards, we were invited to Lund's apartment, where we kept going until four in the morning – quite a wake![22]

Lund still had the energy to run his empire for a few more years, but he died in Sweden in 1954, and his son took over as the country's new carnival king. When it came to efficiency and working his employees hard, he was not far behind his father. Nor did Hans spare himself, never taking time off for holidays. Wherever people gathered in large numbers, at fairs and public exhibitions, Lund's Carnival was there. In a newspaper interview with *Hamar Stiftstidene* in the 1960s, the discussion between the reporter and Hans ran along these lines:

Is carnival a gamble, Lund?

Good weather means more kroner in the till, and I count on sunny days, to put it meteorologically.

We've seen housewives who've used up their husband's weekly wages to play the tombola, and go home happy when they won a half pound of coffee. Is gambling madness very widespread?

I've heard about such cases, but they're purely sporadic. Most folk see it as a sort of popular festival where there is life and movement, colour and music, and I myself think it's better to pay nothing to get in, and wade through the happy crowd, than it is to pay 2 kroner to see a football match between two hick teams.

All your wheels of fortune, carousels, goods bazaars, shooting galleries, sweets booths, the full show, what's its worth in kroner?

Spare me! As if it wasn't enough that the tax authorities never finish asking me about it . . . but a business of that type naturally represents a bit of capital. To put it mildly, I see myself as broke if I don't have 100,000 kroner when I start up a carnival.[23]

Hans had a knack for finance, just like his father, and a nose for good PR stunts. 'The King', as he was called in the carnival world, managed among other things, to get Sonny

Liston, the world champion heavyweight boxer, to come to the country town of Mysen, south-east of Oslo, for a demonstration bout. People shook their heads when they heard what the champion demanded but Hans had the measure of his public. After the fight, the Red Cross, the main organisers, made a large profit. As did Lund.

Hans Lund had realised that it was self-defeating to carry on with old formulas. 'If a carnival is going to be popular, it has to look out for those other attractions, the ones that don't have a sign posted on them saying "This is a gold mine",' he explained once. Old Haakon Lund had understood that when, in 1953, he put the entire collection into storage. After the war, he had continued to tour Sweden with the exhibition, but people were steadily losing interest in it.

In the end he rented a loft in Linköping, Sweden, in which he stored the bizarre collection. Dramatic events followed, when rumours spread through the town that ghosts and mysterious ghost-like figures were restlessly wandering the attic storeroom. Some youths climbed up and broke in, and in a mixture of fear and bravado, they photographed Julia and her son, who were by now in a rather poor condition.

So, the mummies could still attract some attention, but it was less than before. And the other wax cabinet, including its Napoleon, was no longer noteworthy in the postwar world. It was shown once during the 1950s, at Youngstorget in Oslo, rather unsuccessfully. After that, it was exchanged for a large variety tent; it could be folded away, withstood wear and tear better, and took up less space than a collection of wax figures.

But Hans had not the heart to get rid of the Hygienic and Anatomical Exhibition after he had carted it back to Oslo from Linköping. Just occasionally he took it out on the road, for example to the agricultural fair at Ekeberg, on the heights above the centre of Oslo, in the summer of 1959, and 700,000 visited. It was exceptionally warm that summer, and the venereal disease displays went right to the head of sensitive souls but Julia and her son were hardly noticed; they could no longer shock. Hans wanted to keep them, nevertheless; in spite of everything, they were rare objects and they might be valuable one day.

A decade later, in 1969, a telephone rang at the home of the Swedish circus man Trolle Rhodin. Rhodin chatted for a long time and smiled to himself when he hung up. Julia Pastrana? Yes . . . he remembered her well. What on earth had become of her? The call had come from the American judge and politician Roy Mark Hofheinz. A controversial and eccentric figure in American society, he had become well-known as the driving force behind the building of Houston's Astrodome, the world's first roofed stadium, finished in 1965. Hofheinz called the gigantic construction 'the eighth wonder of the world'. Now he was building a hotel in the vicinity, and an 'Astroworld' with room for the largest American circus, the Ringling Brothers and Barnum and Bailey Circus, heir to the legendary P.T. Barnum.

Known for a long time as 'The Greatest Show on Earth', it surpassed all others. Hofheinz was an extremely determined and rich collector of all sorts of rarities who had been in touch with circuses, freak shows and carnivals in and outside the USA for many years. In fact the word 'determined' is a bit of an understatement. He had been mayor of Houston twice in the 1950s, and once had four council members arrested for missing a meeting. On another occasion, he experienced so much internal dissent that he decided that all public officials should be elected a year earlier than the statutes permitted. That move aroused vehement opposition, but Hofheinz pushed his decision through. Soon afterwards he left politics, losing to a stronger opponent, for law and business, and began collecting curiosities to add to his own private chamber of horrors and oddities.

Through his carnival connections, he got wind of a famous hirsute woman, admittedly a stuffed one, that had been a profitable display for many years. Straightaway, he wanted to own her. He would pay whatever it took, but for once that was not enough. Nobody seemed to have any idea where she might be. Hofheinz was in despair.

But Julia had not been completely forgotten, not in Europe at least. In 1963 she became once again an uncomplaining victim of show business, when an Italian-French film co-production *La Donna Scimmia* (*The Ape Woman*) told the sensual and alluring story of a furry young woman, clearly inspired by Julia's life. In the film the woman is found in a convent by an unscrupulous manager who gets her to perform in a bizarre striptease act. Then they marry and she dies giving birth. Afterwards, the woman and child are stuffed, but the audience found this too shocking and the film was not a success. Not even prurient marketing helped. 'No other woman looked like her, felt like her, loved like her', the poster claimed. The description was accurate enough in its way, and maybe it inspired Hofheinz, because he did not give up looking.

Eventually, he heard that Julia had been exhibited in Sweden and Norway, and it was then that he called his closest contact in the Scandinavian entertainment world. Trolle Rhodin was working at that time in the USA as a talent scout for the Greatest Show on Earth. He had started up his own Trolle Rhodin Zoo Circus in 1941, in Gothenburg. It soon become a large enterprise, touring Scandinavia, Germany, Spain, Hungary, Moscow and other countries. The Rhodin family had been jugglers and road people for generations, and deserve a closer look.

The best known was the great nineteenth-century

magician and illusionist 'Professor' Max Alexander, one of the greatest legends in nineteenth-century Scandinavian show business. His son, Max Rhodin, later known on stage as 'Brazil Jack', was a famous pantomime and shadow-show artist. He worked for a long time with the German circus impresario Ernst Renz, about twenty years after Julia Pastrana had toured with a division of Circus Renz. In 1883 Rhodin had an engagement in St Petersburg, in the same period that Theodore Lent and Marie Bartel lived there and exhibited their wax cabinet. It's a small world, the entertainment world. Alexander took on the role of a gypsy, performing as the troubadour Carlo Roodini, and later became the cowboy 'Brazil Jack'. He was described as being 'a very colourful gentleman':

He had a wide, light grey Stetson hat, rolled up on the side like the Texas Rangers. The hat sat at an angle on silky soft, raven black, shoulder-long hair; a Roman nose jutted forth from a chiselled face, [and he wore] a long leather jacket with fringes of light brown leather, . . . green jodhpurs [and] leather leggings with a bunch of buckles. . . . He had plainly modelled himself on Buffalo Bill.[24]

Max was such a big fan of Norway that when the Norwegian patriot and Nobel prize-winning writer Bjørnstjerne Bjørnson died, Rhodin hired a giant silver wreath, engraved with an eight-line eulogy he himself had written. It began thus: 'From Palace and Castle, to Hut thatched with Hay / We miss you so much, oh Son of Norway', and ended with 'Sleep sweetly, great Chieftain, within your Grave / Take thanks for all of the Glory you gave.'

Once, in 1910, Brazil Jack staged a calculated encounter with King Haakon VII of Norway when the king was touring through the Trondheim area. Brazil Jack acted as if he did not know who the King was, and met him in rural surroundings, wearing his full cowboy outfit and accompanied by a tribe of (Swedish) American Indians. King Haakon had a long conversation with him, completely charmed by this unusual Swede who did not know the King's identity. Of course, Rhodin knew full well who he was talking to, and the next day the story was in all the papers. He sought an audience with the King on another occasion, and then the pleasant conversation took place in the royal palace in Oslo.

Max Rhodin ended up as a circus director and father of eight children with names such as Happy Celestino Anselmo, Frantz Xavier, Leonard Haakon Jarl and Barnum Margaretha (the last two being named after the Norwegian ship *Haakon Jarl*, on which his parents had sailed just before his birth, and the circus king P.T. Barnum). His two best-known sons were Teddy, who became chief of ballet at the Malmø City Theatre, and Trolle. So when Trolle Rhodin was asked to find Julia by Hofheinz in Texas, he could pull a lot of strings. The job would be enjoyable, and might make him an unlooked-for profit. Yes, he would find Julia Pastrana, whatever the cost – to Hofheinz, that is.

7

Go Over Her with a Vacuum Cleaner

On 12 September 1969, a large advertisement appeared in the Swedish national newspaper *Dagens Nyheter*. It had been placed by Trolle Rhodin, who had finally admitted to himself that he could not find Julia Pastrana on his own. Reluctantly, he was looking for help. Hofheinz was willing to pay as much as 100,000 kroner for the mummies, and was offering an award of 15,000 kroner to the person who could put him in touch with the owner.

Rhodin got many replies, all from people who had seen Julia in Sweden or Norway during the 1950s. Some remembered her from an agricultural fair in 1959, and others remembered her being stashed away in Linköping. Then Hans Lund contacted him. He had no intention of selling Julia. The price was nowhere near the true worth of the mummy. His message was blunt. He'd rather take Julia on tour than let a rich American get his claws into her. And if he did sell, he'd want more than a hundred thousand. It's cultural history, for God's sake! Hans reckoned he was sitting on a gold mine. Old fox that he was, he wanted to haggle, to squeeze Hofheinz for all he could get. And in any case, he had no need to sell; he had enough money of his own.

And then the newspapers got hold of the story. 'Can you get 150,000 kroner now by selling her to the American?' a journalist from *Hamar Arbeiderblad* asked Hans.[1] 'I wouldn't sell her for that under any circumstances,' Hans answered. 'Naturally, there are others who are interested. It wouldn't surprise me if Madame Tussaud's wanted her. But I might well keep her and show her around Europe again.' The story was rapidly taken up by the national press, and Julia became a hot topic round Swedish and Norwegian breakfast tables.

One still and dark autumn night, two or three fellows entered a warehouse on the east side of Oslo. They felt their way forward between dusty cases, mummies, and misshapen abortions preserved in spirits. One ghost-like apparition after the other turned up before they found what they seek. Careful now! One large box was placed with great care in an car, and driven to a garage, or some other place, in Oslo. All this happened in the early hours of a Tuesday morning, and was to do with moving what might be the most talked-about woman in Norway at that time – Julia Pastrana. 'Once everyone knew that I had Julia Pastrana in my warehouse in Oslo, I no longer dared to keep her there,' the happy owner, carnival director Hans Jæger Lund, told VG. 'In a short while, however, Julia and a lot else from my cabinet of curiosities will be dusted off and put out in the limelight again.'[2]

Hans also told the newspaper VG on 20 September 1969 in the article 'Ape woman on night journey in Oslo. Julia Pastrana in the limelight again. Hans Jæger Lund dusts off his chamber of horrors' that he expected a delegation of bargain-hunters from America. 'But they won't fool me,' he vehemently claimed.

The question of who was fooling whom would not be decided for another six months, but neither Hans nor the newspapers knew that then. And Hofheinz was tearing his hair out in frustration over the stubborn, immovable

Norwegian. When the Swedish newspaper *Expressen* visited
Hans's house on 2 November 1969, Julia and her son were
still stored away in Lund's private garage. Admittedly she
had been shoved right into a corner to make room for a big
black Opel Admiral, a luxury car appropriate for someone of
Lund's status.

Hans complained to the journalist about letters to the
editor from readers demanding that Julia should receive a
proper burial. 'Okay, if they want to bury her, let them do it.
But they've got to pay her true value. Right now, I wouldn't
sell her for a million. I'm thinking about doing business
using her.'[3] And to prove that this was the genuine Julia he
showed people the old Russian embalming document. He
was able in this way to persuade most sceptics that his
claims were true. But, as he said, he did get a visit from one
doubter. 'I had a visit from a man who doubted Julia was
real. He asked me to prise open her jaws so that he could
see her teeth but that would have damaged her. So I lifted
her skirt and said that he should take a look there instead.
Then he no longer doubted any more.' As Hans
pragmatically put it, 'You only need to go over her with a
vacuum cleaner and she's ready to go on show.'

. . . CORPSES OF OLD NORWEGIANS IN CHURCHES

If it was Hans's idea to push the price sky high, he mis-
calculated. He did keep his word and went over Julia with a
hoover before putting her on display in January 1970 but it
was not a success. Stuffed women were no longer in vogue.
This was the age of radicalism and the youth revolution,
and freak shows were not politically correct. At the Expo
Valand fair in Malmø, things came to a head. The
newspapers condemned Julia's display, calling it tasteless
and worse. Even though an employee of Malmø Museum

defended the show, likening it to the relics of Catholic saints, the exhibition was a disaster. Sure, it achieved a great deal of publicity, but financially, it was forced to close. Show business was a balancing act: a bit of a shock, yes, but not too much. And how unfair, Lund could have said, since the Swedes too had a tradition of bearded ladies.

The most famous example is found in a book by the world-famous children's author, Astrid Lindgren. A bearded lady appears in her 1963 book *Emil in the Soup Tureen*. In it, the little scamp Emil visits a large fair at Hultfred Plain, with a circus and carnival, carousel and dance pavilion, sword and fire swallowers. In addition there was 'a splendid lady with a full beard who couldn't swallow anything at all, other than coffee and buns once each hour. She didn't get rich from that, but luckily she had her beard. She could show it for payment, and earn a goodly sum.'[4] Emil doesn't have any money himself, but he is plucky, inventive, and curious, trying as well as he can to trick his way into a free showing.

Then he passed the bearded lady's tent, and saw her through the opening, sitting there and counting her money. She probably wanted to find out how much she had earned off her beard on a single happy day at Hultfred Plain. It wasn't likely to have been any small amount, since she chuckled and stroked her beard in a self-satisfied way. Then she spotted Emil. 'Come in, little boy,' she called. 'You will get to see my beard for nothing at all, because you look like a nice child.' Now, Emil had already seen the beard before, but he was not about to say no to an offer like that. And since it was totally for nothing, he went right into the tent . . . and got at least 25 öre's worth of looking at the beard.

The next minute, they are surprised by a celebrated thief and bandit named the Sparrow. He wants to rob the lady's hard-earned money: 'The bearded lady went white in her face, but not, of course, where she had her beard.'

Emil then saves the situation. He and the lady chase the Sparrow away, and the woman is full of praise for her little rescuer. 'You're really a clever boy,' said the woman with the beard. 'Therefore, you'll get to see my beard as much as you like, for nothing at all.' Emil is however, quite tired, and decides to take the offer as future credit. Keeping in mind Emil's great popularity it is conceivable that many Swedes remembered the story about the bearded lady, even when viewing Julia Pastrana eight years after the book came out. The difference was, of course, that Julia was dead, while Emil's friend was in full bloom. Lindgren's character is active and brave, controlling her own finances. In a nutshell, she has her self-respect intact. Julia was never like that, alive or dead. But now, at least, she was attracting a form of public sympathy, to such an extent that it had an effect on Lund.

Hans no longer knew what the public wanted, and the new spirit of the times came as a surprise to him. Travelling in a carnival you can become isolated from the outside world. But Lund now realised that the most macabre parts of the chamber of horrors should remain in storage for a while longer. He was more uncertain about Julia. He could sell but Hofheinz had just had a brain haemorrhage and, though he survived, his collector's urge was only a shadow of what it had been. According to rumour, his last offer to Hans was for $500,000 before illness took him out of the game. It was a mad, unrealistic amount.

Hans's son Bjørn runs Lund's Tivoli today, thirty years later. He rejects the half-million figure as pure fantasy, and is probably right. Perhaps it was a publicity stunt of Hans's and, if so, he succeeded beyond his dreams. In 1971 he took

Julia on tour round Norway, with a short detour to the Baltic sea archipelago of Åland. According to the newspapers the local ambulances spent all their time running a shuttle service to deal with swooning spectators. The dailies kept the affair in the news, stoking the indignation of their readers, and in consequence crowds turned up to see Julia Pastrana. People wanted to see this disgraceful exhibition for themselves. And so the ape-woman gained for a short time an extra lease of her strange afterlife.

In 1972 Hans was visited by an American colleague, Milton Kauffman, on business in Norway, who got to hear about the furore. He had heard about her vaguely in the past and wanted to have a look at Julia. When Lund showed him the mummy Kauffman could not believe his eyes. He tore off his cowboy hat and slapped it on his thigh. Miss Pastrana was going to America – she just had to.

Kaufmann had contacts with the travelling carnival Gooding's Million Dollar Midways, and reached an agreement with Ruth and Randy Rosenson, who arranged exhibitions of this type and who also ran their own wax museum. Only a few years earlier the World's Strangest Married Couple, the Monkey Girl and the Alligator-Skinned Man, Emmet and Percilla Bejano, had toured with the same company. Hans and his son Bjørn travelled to the USA with Julia as part of their luggage, going first to Florida. There, a customised carnival trailer was built for her by a specialist carnival workshop. Then they took the show on the road north, all the way to New Hampshire. Julia visited Boston again over a century after the first occasion. This time the show kept mainly to country highways, where they would pull in at the larger rest stops and set up banners and advertising posters. A lot of roadshows still use this method. It keeps down the cost of renting local venues, and it makes it easy to move on quickly once local interest has run out.

Eye-catching advertising was crucial once the show was set up, and was provided by a team of banner painters. Many banner painters specialised in travelling freakshows; most were based in Florida, and they weren't short of work. With a well-developed sense of fantasy and exaggeration, their yards-long banners proclaimed such attractions as the Two-Headed Racoon, the Cyclops Pig with Elephant Trunk, Barracuda-Ape, Penguin Boy, the Toad Man with Two Noses, the Woman with Alligator Skin, and the Man with Two Faces. And now the time had come to proclaim Julia Pastrana and her son. They were exhibited with accompanying scientific descriptions of their history and their abnormality. This was to give the show an air of respectability, not that this mattered to those members of the American public who pulled off the freeway to take a look. Some paid the admission fee to the trailer, but fewer than Lund hoped for, and not enough to cover his preliminary expenses: freight costs, plane tickets, trailers and all the rest. And Hans had to split the takings with the American organisers. So the profits were nothing to write home about.

The big problem of course, was that Julia was not 'Alive!' 'Alive' was the declaration in large painted letters on almost all the banners advertising these roadside attractions. There were certainly some swindles. A Cyclops pig with an elephant's trunk? Unlikely! But the banner said it was 'Alive!' If the public were disappointed when they saw some poor one-eyed pig with a trunk glued on its snout, too bad – they'd paid their money. Julia was genuine but she wasn't alive. She had the air of a museum piece, and this didn't fit the mood of 1970s America. Nevertheless, the trip continued to Milwaukee, Indiana and then south to Florida. Hans and Bjørn decided perhaps it would be a safer bet to go on tour in Scandinavia, but the public mood was changing there as well.

The following paragraph appeared in an Oslo newspaper in March 1973:

Five private individuals in Oslo have asked Bishop Reidar Kobro to intervene to stop the planned tour in Sweden of the embalmed corpse of the Ape Woman Julia Pastrana and her son. Kobro asked the Ministry of Justice to deliver the bodies to the Norwegian authorities for cremation or burial. The mummies are owned today by a Norwegian carnival director, who has traipsed around several American cities with them, displaying them for money.[5]

Norwegian moralists had had more than enough of the Lund chamber of horrors, and were preparing to launch a large campaign. Lund, busy preparing the show to go on the road, did not realise what he was up against, and brushed the problem aside as laughable. However, this time the authorities became involved, even though they were unclear about their role in all this. The paper *Aftenposten* reported:

The Ministry of Justice has transferred the documents in the case to the Office of Church Affairs in the Department of Church and Education, which will take a position on the matter, to the degree that it falls under the responsibility of that same Department.

Assistant Secretary Guttorm Queseth at the Office of Church Affairs told *Aftenposten* that the matter was not the concern of his Office. Cremations and burials that concerned the Office are those connected with the newly deceased. In this instance, it seemed to him difficult to say who in what department had the 'natural' jurisdiction.

Nor did Assistant Secretary Kjell Lund-Johansen in the Ministry of Justice, who first had the case for consideration, have any clue. 'There aren't any rules for cases like this. It's totally unique,' he told *Aftenposten*. 'The case does not involve displays in Norway where we have permission to exhibit Egyptian mummies and corpses of old Norwegians in churches.'[6]

There were no precedents for a case like this. In the government departments everyone was scratching his head, not wanting to have anything to do with it. Did it really matter what happened to these old bones? As the assistant secretary said, there were other cases of embalmed corpses in Norwegian churches, in Norderhov church in Ringerike county, for example. There, the bodies of priest Jonas Ramus and his wife Anna Colbjørnsdatter lay on display in the crypt, with parchment-like skin, sunken eyes and unpleasantly bared teeth.

Anna had become one of Norway's few national heroines in 1716 when she single-handedly duped a large group of Swedish soldiers during the Great Northern War. The priest Ramus was at that time an old, sick man who, according to legend, hid himself in the cellar.[7] Later, both were embalmed. 'This is a proper Man, book-learned,' explains a document from 1690. True, but in his glass coffin, 250 years after his death, no one could pretend he was a pretty sight. But this did not become a matter of debate until the mid-1990s, after Ringerikes Museum put a T-shirt on sale featuring an image of the embalmed Ramus. Just the sort of clever marketing that a carnival king would admire.

The same moral fault-line was exposed in both these controversies. In 1973, Bishop Kobro spoke to *Aftenposten*: It is correct that one can view corpses in this country, both in museums and in churches, but in this case I react to a woman and her dead child being exploited for economic gain after their death. One could claim that people pay to go into museums to view corpses, but this is a question of feelings of respect.[8]

The carnival director was not in the habit of listening to criticism from outsiders, but this brouhaha about Julia was becoming a burden for the 62-year-old Hans. He seemed not to be concerned by the fuss, but no one likes being accused of using the dead to line his pockets. He liked the know-alls even less. They could take a running jump. No one was going to get their claws into Julia while he was alive!

. . . THIS HERE IS AWFULLY MACABRE!

In spring 1973 the mummies were hired out to Björkmans Tivoli in Arboga for a new tour in Sweden. As in the 1850s, Julia was presented as a cross between an ape and a human, which at first was taken simply as something rather amusing, a bit titillating. But when the carnival came to Hudiksvall, north of Stockholm, in September, it was greeted with a banning order by the health authorities. Corpses could no longer be exhibited for the sake of profit, for aesthetic and hygienic reasons. The Swedish Minister of Justice, Lennart Gejer, became involved and declared that Julia – and all other dead people – were not welcome. From then on the dead either went into the earth or a museum. If they were Norwegian, then they must leave Sweden immediately. Hans was beginning to get tired of it all. And when the Norwegian authorities decided that they would also prohibit the exhibition, things looked even worse.

The Carnival King was no longer in top form after a bout of heart problems the year before and began to toy with the idea of pulling out. In 1971, he had already said, 'I'm fed up to here with the carnival. I think the whole mess is beginning to stink, and I've actually had more than enough.

Now I've got my son up and running; I've made a passable carnival man out of him, even though that takes time, because it's not easy work. So I want to pull back and enjoy my evening years.'[9]

Of course, it didn't turn out that way. The old showman didn't give up his life's work, nor did he want his opponents to win the battle for the mummies. Meanwhile, Julia's self-appointed champion, Bishop Kobro, was not satisfied with the exhibition clampdown. He argued that Julia and her son should have been confiscated by the state and given a proper burial. Lund replied that if the bishop wanted to bury mummies, let him go to Egypt! With that, he declared the debate over and put Julia back in storage. She rested there in peace for three years.

Then, in April 1974, Hans appeared in the columns of *VG*: 'Of course there's going to be a carnival again this year. We're setting it up, down at the sand pit at Lilletorget at Grønland [in central Oslo] and it'll stand there in all its glory, nice and ready. And so I, with Scandinavia's largest travelling carnival – when we have every bit and piece it fills up 70 railway wagons. At Lilletorget we've only obtained the space to set up 25 per cent of the equipment – stupid or what?'[10]

The carnival king did not feel bitter towards the authorities because of the lack of exhibition sites and the prohibition on the mummies. Instead, with princely magnanimity, Hans proposed making the east Central Station area into a permanent carnival site. He himself would provide all the equipment. 'The city can use all my gear – Hans Lund's Carnival Foundation, or something like that – doesn't it have a nice sound to it?'[11]

But he died in 1976, a showman to the end. His son Bjørn took over the family firm with its carousels, bumper cars, tombolas, wax displays and mummies. One night that same year someone broke into the carnival warehouse at

Rommen, a deserted industrial area in eastern Oslo, between Romsås and Stovner, with their high-rise council flats.

Thirteen-year-old Tore Skofterød and his three friends had become curious about a giant warehouse of corrugated iron. This was by no means their first escapade: petty lawbreaking was a regular part of their hunt for excitement. The building was arched, like a hangar, with great wooden shutters barring the doors and windows, and difficult to enter. The teenagers managed to bend up one of the metal plates closest to the ground and peered in.

They couldn't believe their luck. They saw go-carts and bumper cars in shiny colours, and then enlarged the opening so that they could roll them out. But they couldn't get them running. 'There were go-carts all over Rommen but we couldn't start up a single one,' said Skofterød twenty-six years later. And they couldn't run the bumper cars either – naturally enough since they run on electricity. So there was nothing else to do but to go on a treasure hunt – and the place was full of all kinds of things. They soon found a glass case with two human-like forms inside. They broke open the case and took out the figures, thinking that they must be some type of mannequin.

'It was my friend Torgeir who ripped her arm off. It was hairy but nonetheless smooth and fine on the outside and full of wood-wool inside. The child was rather large for a baby, but very worn and a shambles. He appeared to have been eaten by mice and rats. We never dreamed they were actual people!'[12] Skofterød could still vividly remember that remarkable night twenty-six years later.

They took the arm out of the hangar, and tried again to start the go-carts. Suddenly a police car appeared, blue lights flashing. The boys ran, dropping everything except, of course, the brown arm from the doll in the glass case. Torgeir showed the arm to his older brother once he got

home, who immediately realised that it was human and
called the Grønland police station in central Oslo. The police
came out and picked up the arm, and the brothers said they
had just found it somewhere. The police generously viewed
the matter as a boyish prank, and did not follow it up.

The next day, the boys returned to the carnival
warehouse and broke in once more, but Julia and her son
had gone. The police had taken her away, and Tore and
Torgeir shivered from delight mixed with fright. Afterwards,
they suffered from bad consciences. It was difficult to forget
the bearded woman and her mouse-gnawed son.

The police forgot the whole thing quickly – nothing, after
all, had been stolen. The go-carts were collected and rolled
back inside the hangar. Julia was taken into the police car,
and the metal plates were nailed back into place. The stuffed
baby was falling to pieces by now, partly as a result of the
break-in, so it was simply thrown in the rubbish. Julia was
stashed away in the police headquarters' cellar at Grønland,
and no one thought of notifying the owner. Who owned her
anyway? It was a dead person, after all!

Anyone would think that long-dead bodies were an
extremely rare sight in the West in 1976, but in December
that year, a frightening find was made in Long Beach,
California. Hanging from the roof of a haunted fairground
ride, called Laff-in-the-Dark, was a full-sized dummy, spray-
painted fluorescent orange, strung up by the neck with a
noose – a hanged man. A blue light shone on it, giving the
sinister dangling figure a spooky aura. People riding past in
the small carriages shrieked at the mannequin's grinning
teeth and rail-thin, naked body, then forgot about it and
moved on to the next thrill. But one day a Universal Studios
television team visited Laff-in-the-Dark while location-
hunting for the series *The Six Million Dollar Man*, featuring
the bionically modified superhero Colonel Steve Austin who

went round chasing foreign spies and international criminals. Laff-in-the-Dark looked like an ideal location for an episode called 'Carnival of Spies'.

On the day of filming, one of the production team went up for a closer look at the spray-painted hanging man. The dummy clearly weighed very little, swaying in the slight breeze, and they reckoned it was made from papier-mâché. Then another crew member went up to it and grabbed hold of one arm. He jumped when the limb fell off, and he got a horrid creepy feeling when he examined the arm more closely. Papier-mâché it was not.

It was quickly determined that it was in fact a corpse, a desiccated male mummy. But whose? After much wide-ranging detective work, the corpse was identified as Elmer McCurdy, a failed petty criminal and robber who was shot and killed after committing what has been called one of the USA's most unsuccessful train robberies. After his death, Elmer was pumped full of arsenic and embalmed to be put on display – for paying customers – at the Joseph Johnson Funeral Home in Pawhuska, Oklahoma. Whisked away afterwards by men purporting to be relatives, his remains were exhibited as a 'Real Dead Outlaw' over the entire country for several decades. He lay for a long time in a coffin with screws mounted in his neck and feet so that via an ingenious system he could be made to shake himself, profitably scaring passing spectators. Louis Sonney's Museum of Crime was one of the stops along his posthumous way because, found in the mouth of the mummy, was a 1924 coin and a ticket from the Sonney museum. It was partly from such evidence that Elmer's background was pieced together, a life that in its brutal brevity was described thus: 'Born 1880. Shot dead 1911. Buried 1977.' And rediscovered, one might add, because of a ripped-off arm in an amusement centre in 1976. The lives of Elmer McCurdy and Julia Pastrana were as different as could be, but in death they suffered a remarkably similar weird fate, except that the one-armed Julia was not laid to rest but stored in a police cellar.

It was a long time before Bjørn Lund discovered that anything was missing from his storage centre. The warehouse was crammed with faulty and superfluous items and nothing was in order. Eventually, in 1979, Lund discovered that Julia and her son were missing. Not until then were the police notified about this strange case. Stuffed woman stolen. Age 145 years. Distinguishing marks: full beard and silk dress. But the police had completely forgotten about the insignificant break-in, and soon put the case on ice. Memories of Julia were also on ice. For ten years, Lund's Carnival continued to tour, and no one missed the Ape Woman. Neither the public nor Lund himself were aware that Julia's body had in fact been long since recovered. Then in February 1990 Julia's story hit the headlines again. The crime magazine *Kriminal Journalen* reported that she had been found in the underground department of the Institute for Forensic Medicine in Oslo.

Here, right in the centre of the city, Julia had lain undisturbed in a very damaged state ever since the police had deposited her just a few months after the theft. She had been discovered in a very damaged state, in the forensic collection, by journalists from the magazine. They now wanted to photograph her, but permission had to be obtained from the Grønland Police Station. It was the police who had delivered her to the hospital, and therefore they must hold the rights for photograph permissions – since no one had bothered to report the find to Bjørn Lund. But there was a legal grey area: who did have the ownership rights over a corpse? And can a dead person be owned by someone, or does it revert to the state when found by the police? Bjørn Lund never put in a claim to recover Julia's body, after he heard about the case from the crime magazine. He was puzzled that he had not been notified when the body was first recovered. But really, it didn't make much difference – Julia's time had passed. Carnivals could no longer be based on freaks, living or otherwise.

He did take care of her specially built Russian carriage though, which was moved to the southern coastal city of Stavanger with the rest of the business. As of February 2003, Julia's handsome carriage was still stashed away, with its now worn wooden trimmings and faded silk, in a crowded trailer at a storage depot on the outskirts of the town.

When the magazine tried the police, Oslo's chief of police Willy Haugli was totally surprised to hear about the Institute for Forensic Medicine. 'No, she isn't staff – she's stuffed!' the reporter explained patiently.[13] 'What the bloody . . . it sounds totally macabre, this thing!' replied Haugli. Later, after the request to take photographs, the magazine received a short reply from Haugli's office: 'After due consideration, the Oslo Police have found that they cannot give permission for photography. We are of the opinion that the woman should be left to rest in peace.' No one could argue with that, not *Kriminal Journalen* anyway, who said Julia's situation was like a game of musical chairs. But her wandering would soon be over. The affair was now in the hands of the bureaucrats.

In November 1993, Julia's case was taken up by *Aftenposten*, which carried a long article headed 'Wolf Woman Julia should go to a new museum'. A decision had been made to establish a medical history museum in Oslo, possibly connected to the new National Hospital at Gaustad on the west side of town. There were plans to display over 100,000 objects, including human material and Julia. In the medical collections there were eight so-called changelings, mis-shapen people born in nineteenth-century

Norway, who'd been pickled in alcohol for scientific research. One of them was the extremely overweight woman called Swamp Maren who, it was rumoured, had been embalmed in her own fat.

A committee of enquiry was established to advise the government about the difficult and delicate Pastrana affair, and it was decided that a museum would be the best solution. As Professor Sokolov once said about Julia, 'Wherever they might be, they have a claim upon the scientific world.'[14] The Ministry of Justice regarded dead individuals as not having owners, but said in an official communication that they could be 'in principle taken over in ownership by those who find themselves in possession of the object'.[15] In other words, Julia was an object, just as she always had been for the people around her. 'I personally cannot see any ethical reservations against keeping remains, nor any religious [ones]. . . . A dead body should certainly be treated with respect, but that could be achieved through discreet storage,' Olav Hilmar Ivarsen, Professor of Pathology of the University of Oslo, told the press.

However, when ethics and religion are involved, matters can become complicated. One year after the decision to establish a museum, the case took a new turn. On 22 November 1994, at 9 a.m. precisely, a long and wide-ranging discussion commenced in the Academic Collegium at the University of Oslo. Twenty-two cases were under consideration, one of the last – official designation 94/1693 – being the 'Remains of Julia Pastrana'. One of the Collegium's members, Lita Scheen, proposed: 'Julia Pastrana shall not be buried.' There were factions at the university that wanted to retain her for research, and burial was seen by some as scientific sacrilege. The proposal, however, was rejected by nine votes to three.

By now, the meeting had been in session for over six

hours, and the honourable academicians, including Lucie Smith, nationally known jurist and University Rector, were discreetly yawning. They had been dealing with such weighty matters as 'Rental of up to two floors' office space in the new sports facility' and 'Annulment of the arrangement for partial recommendation of the students' expenditures for typewriting masters' theses and their equivalent'; the Collegium's enthusiasm for further debate was on the wane.

Another committee member put forward another proposal more to people's liking: 'The Collegium has evaluated the case of Julia Pastrana's fate in light of the enquiry of the Church, Education, and Research Department. After totally weighing the ethical and research-related aspects, the Collegium recommends that Julia Pastrana be buried after a tissue sample is procured for future DNA analysis. The University's Rector is asked to clarify future responsibility in the matter with the department.'[16] This was something everyone could live with, including the press and critical opinion demanding a worthy end for Julia. It would ease the complaints of the public. And the Department wanted to resolve this unpleasant business. Everyone seemed to be happy. Now they could work through the rest of the day's agenda. Passed unanimously! Plant her in the ground instead of displaying her, and the problem will go away for good. But it was not going to be that easy!

The Ape Woman had aroused the concern of many lay people, bureaucrats, and researchers. They protested vehemently against the planned burial; the case was far from over. The press used up much ink on it. 'This is a very emotional matter, and there hasn't been an easy solution,' a political adviser said to VG in 1996.[17] So the plans were changed yet again. Now Julia would be kept in situ, after an intervention by Church and Educational Minister Gudmund

Hernes. He was one of the Social Democrat government's
most powerful and effective ministers. With a doctorate in
sociology, he was also a powerful speaker. Many saw him as
power-hungry and arrogant; however, he was known for
getting things done. The decision on Julia had been made
before he changed departments and became Minister of
Health in 1995. A year later, the matter was settled once
and for all. Julia's fate was child's play for a minister of his
calibre, who had once been a researcher himself, not to
mention foreman for the colleges and universities board.
The affair went the way science wanted it to go. A member
of the official project said to *Aftenposten*: 'The woman is a
cultural-historical treasure, and a medical curiosity, and
therefore has a general value in preservationist terms. But
she is also connected with a specific rare illness syndrome,
which makes her worthy of display.'[18]

The same year, *Dagbladet* proclaimed on its pages: 'Ape
Woman from Mexico likely to be buried there.' Confusion
was total. A Norwegian woman had presented herself to the
authorities, claiming surprisingly to be the rightful owner of
Julia's earthly remains. That didn't fit well with the
Department's definition of ownership, but it was always
worth a try. 'Ape Woman burial probably at birthplace,'
Dagbladet reported optimistically. As if anyone had the
faintest idea where she had been born. There was, of
course, no burial, nor, on the other hand, any display in a
museum. The University newspaper *Uniform*, no. 17, 1999,
reported 'Julia Pastrana rests in peace', as she had done for
the past two years, at the Schreiner Collection of the
Institute Group for Medical Basal Subjects at Gaustad. It was
in fact here at Gaustad, in the west of Oslo, that the
country's new national hospital was being built, the
nation's pride both in treatment of patients and research.
The building complex was a logical investment for a society

that is among the world's richest; the country wanted, naturally, to showcase its own medical expertise. The physical plant of the National Hospital is appropriately enormous; its construction cost about £450,000,000. The architects described it as 'the humanistic hospital', and the contrast with the previous national hospital – a sad, run-down, and unhygienic concrete pile in the middle of Oslo – is almost inconceivable. The country could no longer countenance anything of the sort in an enlightened age. But certain things do not change: the dead, least of all.

'It's no different than the other thousands of dead churchly individuals preserved in sarcophagi all over the entire world,' said the Medical Institute Manager Gunnar Nico-laysen to the university newspaper about his famous guest Julia Pastrana.[19] 'There is climate control in the room where she rests,' he added reassuringly. Mummies do well in such surroundings, and he was careful to emphasise that it was the Department and not the Institute that had asked for her to be there. It was all very dignified, he finally pointed out, while the University newspaper optimistically warranted that here she would lie 'for several hundred years'.

The managing director of the Schreiner Collection, Peter Holck, stated in a telephone conversation of February 2003 that Julia has rested totally undisturbed up to now. No X-ray examination, no DNA analysis. Nothing at all. He believed that little of her skeleton was intact, other than the skull. But neither he nor other experts knew for sure. Perhaps she would be examined at some future moment, perhaps not. Who knows? 'I've been at this for over forty years,' Holck said, 'and if there's one thing I'm sure of, it's that current knowledge dates rapidly. Methods and needs are changing all the time. We therefore cannot exclude the possibility that in the future, we could derive great utility from Julia Pastrana's genetic material, her DNA.'

The researchers had spoken, science had won. Julia Pastrana was removed from the old Pathology Building's dark cellar to the new National Hospital in Oslo. There, within the citadel of modern medicine, in a large glass sarcophagus not unlike that which she shared with her son for more than a century, would she lie.

A wandering body, laid to rest. A journey done.

As recently as autumn and winter 2002, a highly unusual play about Julia's life made an impression on audiences when it toured parts of England and Scotland. *The True History of the Tragic Life and Triumphant Death of Julia Pastrana* by Shaun Prendergast was performed totally in the dark, both on stage and in the theatre hall itself, to the mixed enjoyment, apparently, of the public. The piece showed in any case a willingness to regard Julia's life and death from a new angle, both title and performance-wise. But you would have to be in show business to understand how any part of Julia's tragic death could in any way be claimed to be 'triumphant'. Then again, show business was her life. And afterlife. The Ape Woman is dead, the show goes on.

Notes

A note on sources

Julia Pastrana has always been an object of fascination, and many have written about her throughout the years. The accounts can be divided into several broad categories: promotional materials from show business, scientific writings, articles in newspapers and magazines, and articles and mentions in books about 'freaks'.

Much uncertainty surrounds the life of Julia Pastrana and sources are, to put it mildly, imprecise and often contradictory; this is hardly surprising given that Julia worked in a business permeated by exaggeration and lies. In addition, the lives of poor, malformed Indians and travelling artists of the 1800s are not easy to trace now, a century and a half later.

This book is the first to present Julia Pastrana and her life as its main theme. Our most important sources were the following, in chronological order: Sokolov [Sukolov] (1862), Buckland (1866), Saltarino (1895), Hutchinson (1900), Miles (1973), Drimmer (1973), Mannix (1976), Bondeson (1992) and Snigurowicz (1999).

We were able to find a few sources in Norway, some in various archives, and some from the private collections of show enthusiasts, but during the writing we discovered that carnivals and 'freaks' are only sparsely covered by Norwegian resources. The USA had more to offer. Bogdan (1988) provides a particularly good insight into the business. Among our written sources, Jan Bondeson is undoubtedly the most important. The London-based Swedish doctor and author has worked hard to publicise Julia Pastrana's fate and has uncovered new, exciting material. No one has previously written so comprehensively about Julia as

Bondeson, in a series of articles and books. Just as he has to a large degree built upon earlier sources, so we have been inspired by him and his predecessors. To paraphrase, 'All biographers stand on others' shoulders, and we have not stood at the bottom.'

One: A Sympathetic, Intelligent Monster

1. 'Root-digger Indians' – a diffuse term, somewhat derogatory, used by white English speakers from very early on. It did not refer to any specific American Indian group, but was indiscriminately applied to natives of widely varying cultures encountered by the European settlers of the North American continent. The reference is clearly to those who had to rely on roots, tubers and other plant material to supplement their diet, particularly in areas where food was difficult to obtain. With the arrival in California of the Forty-Niners, the terms 'Diggers' or 'Digger Indians' were used to describe the Seed-Gatherers of California and the Great Basin between the Rocky Mountains and the Sierra Nevada. This was a common designation for several different ethnic groups who, unable to practise agriculture because of the harsh, dry climate, wandered from camp to camp in search of game and edible plants. Despite their ethnic and cultural distinctions, these groups were lumped together under a name that reflected their similar economies. Strictly speaking, the term 'Digger Indians' for Julia's unidentified tribe is inaccurate because current research restricts the term to Californian tribes. Our use of 'root-digger Indians' is taken from Bondeson who, in turn, has derived it from Julia's contemporary promotional material. As such, it probably represents the furthest southern extension of a popular folk term.

2. The description of Julia's birth is based upon accounts of Indian customs in north-west Mexico (cf. Lumholtz and others).

3. Mexico's indigenous inhabitants, the descendants of the Aztecs, were originally named *nahual*. The Spanish used the

term from early on (see Steck, 1951). Julia Pastrana possibly belonged to this group. Their language was Nahuatl. A *nagual* (from the Nahuatl word 'to disguise' is, in some Indian tribes, a guardian spirit for each human individual. Nagualism (from the Aztec *naualli*) was a widespread belief that special people, for example shamans, could transform themselves into animals to carry out unpleasant acts. There are examples of nagualism in North, Central and South America (see entries for *nagualism* and *animalism* in *Encyclopaedia Britannica, Micropedia*, 1974 edn).

4. Julia's earliest childhood is cloaked in obscurity. One untrustworthy source states that she was sold into show business by her parents, another says that she was left to die in the forest but survived, and the third version is the one we have presented in this book. Julia's stay with Governor Sanchéz in Sinaloa probably did occur, and was referred to in show material from the 1850s.

Crumine and Weigand's research concerning the Indians of north-west Mexico has been of great use, as has that of Lumholtz in spite of his, by modern standards, unsophisticated, popular style.

5. Lucca, an ancient town in Tuscany, has in its cathedral of San Martino an ancient wooden effigy (claimed to have arrived in the city in the eighth century) of the crucified Christ, called *Santo Volto* (Holy Face), the head of which is supposed to have been carved by angels. The famous cult figure, clad in rich robes of full length, is venerated three times each year. During the Middle Ages, the Santo Volto of Lucca was a focus of European pilgrimages. Devotion was widespread throughout the Christian world, with chapels dedicated to it appearing in cities as far apart as Madrid, Vienna, Vilnius and London.

Two: The Mysterious Animal

1. A broad understanding of the city of New York in the 1800s may be obtained from Lyman.

2. Bogdan, p. 226.
3. This show name was also used by the famous bearded lady Annie Jones who at just twelve months old, was exhibited as 'Infant Esau' in 1866. She was later known as 'Esau Child', and later still as 'Esau Lady'. It comes as no surprise that it was P.T. Barnum who made her famous, and who gave her the name.
4. Parker, pp. 88–91.
5. For a detailed and comprehensive overview of the 'Cardiff Giant' swindle and its influence up to the present day, see Tribble's 'Giants in the Head'.
6. Snyder, p. 9.
7. There remains much controversy about the ultimate fate of the famous warrior's head. For a summary of the various opinions, see Wickman, and also Orlean's chapter, 'Osceola's Head'.
8. Bondeson, 1997, p. 219.
9. Snigurowicz is a very good, well-documented source for understanding the nineteenth-century view of apes, 'freaks' and bearded ladies, including Julia Pastrana. *Men and Apes* (Morris and Morris) is interesting for its broad historical perspective of our concepts of apes, even though Julia is not mentioned in it, and it is the source of the quotations from Beccari and Bontius.
10. Lent's name appears in Frost ('Mr. Lent is Lessee and manager in New York'), p.223. The same writer also mentions P.T. Barnum's promotional materials on, among others, the Digger Indians (pp. 197–200).

Three: An Offence Against All Propriety

1. Henry James, in Best, p. 27.
2. John Simon, in Best, p. 27.
3. Bondeson, 1997, p. 221.
4. Ibid., p. 221.
5. Ibid., p. 222.
6. Ibid., p. 222.

7. The earliest and most important source for understanding Julia's personality and habits is without question Saltarino.

8. Munby, pp. 5–13. The poet Arthur Munby (1828–1910) was a failed lawyer turned civil servant. One of many Victorian men fascinated by lower-class women (George Gissing was another), he was obsessed by them and eventually married his maid in secret. His regular acquaintances included Ruskin, Rossetti and Thackeray, and he knew many other important figures from the higher social, political, intellectual and artistic echelons of late Victorian times. He left behind thousands of letters and interviews dealing with working-class females, detailing their lives, habits, wages and much more, which are kept today at the Trinity College Library at Cambridge.

   Given his Pastrana poem and the stated circumstances of its writing, one might guess that she represented the epitome of wild animal sexuality which he found so attractive and threatening. Sublimating these feelings, he channelled them into his sociological work.

9. Gould and Pyle, pp. 228–30.

10. Rasch, p. 461.

11. Ibid., p. 461.

12. The genetic and cellular explanation of the development of hypertricosis is thoroughly explained in Leroi (2003), pp. 276–80.

13. Francis Trevelyan Buckland (1826–80) drifted from medicine to natural history, becoming government inspector of fisheries. He wrote numerous books on natural history and scientific pisciculture. In Bompas (c. 1914) there are interesting day-to-day notes about Bucklands whereabouts, concerning the meeting with Julia Pastrana, and him writing about her, among other things.

14. Buckland, 1866, pp. 44–6.

15. Darwin, vol. 1, p. 328.

16. Miles, p. 162. Miles is best on Julia's teeth, and is currently the best documented source on her in general. Bondeson and Miles described her genetic condition in a detailed fashion in their co–authored article.

17. Treves, pp. 1–2.

18. Ibid., pp. 2–3.

19. Ibid., p. 4.

20. There are several books written about, or concerning in part, Joseph Merrick, the 'Elephant Man' (1862–90). We have taken Treves's book as our reference point because it preserves the period atmosphere used in this book. The first book to deal with Merrick at length, it provides a first-hand account of him (and his and Julia's times). Howell and Ford reprint Treves's essay in their book.

21. Howell and Ford, p. 203.

22. Bogdan, p. 154.

23. Barbara Urslerin – this surname is found in two different forms. We use the same version as does Bondeson (2000), derived from an early German print by Isaac Bruun. The authors have, however, during their visit to the National Fairground Archive in Sheffield, found an old English print (published by William Richardson, Castle Street, Leicester Fields, and reproduced in this book), which gives her name as 'Barbara Urselin'. This English depiction of Barbara is very similar to the German, and is probably a copy of it. We have kept to Urslerin, since the German print seems to have precedence, being more authentic.

24. John Evelyn, quoted in Bondeson 2000, p. 1.

25. Brackenhofer, cited in Bondeson 2000, p. 2.

26. This quotation, and the following analysis of Julia's presence in France, is derived from Snigurowicz.

27. For the French text of *La femme à barbe*, see Snigurowicz, note 39.

28. This quotation appears in Otto, p. 123.

29. Ibid., pp. 123–4.

Four: The Embalmed Female Nondescript

1. Leo Tolstoy, *Khromov*, p. 95.

2. Sokolov, p. 467. Concerning the embalming of Julia and her son, see Miles, but first and foremost Sokolov. Sokolov's name

is sometimes given as Sukolov. We have kept to his name as given in the *Lancet*.

3. Sokolov, p. 467.

4. Ibid., p. 467.

5. Natron is a hydrous sodium carbonate occurring naturally in surface deposits in Egypt.

6. Felix Dzerzhinsky, as quoted in Zbarsky and Hutchinson, p. 16. Lenin had placed Dzerzhinsky in charge of the Cheka, the first Soviet secret police service, in 1917.

7. Nadezhda Krupskaya, as quoted in Zbarsky and Hutchinson, p. 15.

8. Ibid., p. 27.

9. V.N. Rozanov, as quoted in Zbarsky and Hutchinson, p. 82.

10. Ibid., p. 86.

11. Fertridge, as quoted in Zbarsky and Hutchinson, p. 91.

12. Sokolov, p. 468–9.

13. Ibid., p. 468.

14. Hunter's collection was bequeathed to the University of Glasgow, where it is displayed in the Hunterian Museum.

15. Thompson, p. 165.

16. Ibid., p. 166.

17. Several sources, including Bondeson (1992, p. 267), state that Julia was exhibited in 1862 at the stately mansion Burlington House in Westminster. This is factually incorrect. Both the *Lancet* (15 March 1862), where the Piccadilly address is given the first time, while the exhibition was taking place, and Miles (1973) are reliable on this point.

18. Buckland, in Miles, p. 163.

19. Quotation in Bondeson, 1992, p. 266.

20. Otto, p. 124.

21. Ibid., p. 125.

22. Ibid., pp. 125–6.

Five: An Extremely Remarkable Hairiness

1. Otto, p. 126.

2. 'A case in point', p. 222.

3. Charles Reade (1814–84), English novelist and dramatist, best remembered for his historical romance *The Cloister and the Hearth*. For a while the Sinclair Lewis of his day, he wrote several novels which were intended to expose social injustices. His writing methods involved the mining (like his character Mr Rolfe) of his notebooks, which he filled with vast quantities of description and data regarding human nature, from his own observations, newspapers, travel accounts and official documents. We assume his mention of Julia Pastrana derives from these notes.

4. Reade, vol. II, p. 163.

5. Ibid., vol. II, p. 164.

6. Ibid., vol. II, p. 166.

7. 'Une enfant velue', p. 384. For French text, see Snigurowicz, note 9. The 'Monsieur Keane' mentioned was Augustus H. Keane (1833–1912), professor and author of *Ethnology* [Cambridge,1896], *Man Past and Present* [Cambridge, 1899], etc.

8. Lumholtz, vol. II, p. 470.

9. Lumholtz, vol. I, p. xiv.

10. Ibid., pp. 192–3.

11. Ibid., pp. 70–1.

Six: A Cultural and Historical Treasure

1. Norway's capital has changed names several times. From the early 1600s, when the country was under the Danish crown, until 1877 (well after Norway had joined in union with Sweden in 1814), the city was named Christiania after the Danish King Christian IV (1577–1648). From 1877 to the mid-1920s it was spelt 'Kristiania', but from 1925 onwards it has been called Oslo. Oslo is the town's original Norwegian name, pre-dating the Danish rule.

2. This description of Lund is from the autobiography of Arne Arnardo, Norwegian circus king, as cited in Ødegaard, pp. 110–11. While still slim and unknown, Arnardo was once employed as a balance artist and aerialist with Lund's Tivoli,

under the stage name *Der Rote Teufel* – The Red Devil. It is clear that Arnardo, who came in his older years to resemble Lund, had great respect for his predecessor.

3. Article, *Social-Demokraten*, Oslo, 1921. The advertisement in *Social-Demokraten* is here mentioned and reproduced for the first time since its publication in 1921.

4. The newspaper advertisement for the Hartkopfian Panopticon (see p.109) has not been reproduced anywhere since it was printed in *Aftenposten* in 1899. Our source here is Berthelsen who, through patient detective work, dug up this information in the dusty archives of the National Library of Norway, mentioning it in his book. The information that Julia visited Norway before 1921 is unmentioned by Bondeson and all others.

5. Mentioned in an article in the Oslo newspaper *VG*, 27 November 1993.

6. As the alert reader may notice, there are still some existing discrepancies regarding this point. Julia was claimed to have been embalmed, yet in her current state appears at some time to have been stuffed, at least in part, with the easily observable evidence of wood-wool or batting bulging out at various points of her worn anatomy. Was Julia first embalmed, and later partly stuffed? How does an embalmed corpse obtain the rigidity needed to be displayed without any visible support, standing, as Julia was observed to have been, from the earliest days of her posthumous career, at least from 1862 onwards? All this is further evidence that many mysteries regarding Julia remain to be solved.

7. Thomson, p. 266.

8. Ibid., p. 265.

9. Ibid., p. 266

10. Muus, as cited in Waage, p. 31.

11. Waage. p. 31.

12. Ilboe, p. 125.

13. Ibid., p. 125.

14. The Spanish Cape was an instrument of punishment. It was an ambulatory version of the stocks, shaped like a large

inverted tub, covering the upper body and arms of the victim inside so that only head and legs were showing. The unfortunate wearer of this contraption was then forced to parade around in public.

15. Ilboe, p. 146.
16. Lerfald, unpublished manuscript.
17. Ibid.
18. Ibid.
19. Josef Terboven (1898–1945) was the German Nazi *Reichscommissar* for Norway, and was probably, after Quisling, the most hated man in the country during the occupation. He committed suicide at the end of the war.
20. It has not been possible to document the information about Lund's clash with Müller. Bondeson is the source of the story, but neither the Norwegian State Archives (*Riksarkivet*), who searched both Norwegian and German archives on our request, nor the Military Museum (*Forsvarsmuseet*) in Oslo were able to confirm it. That is not particularly important, however, since the event could well have taken place even though details are sketchy and documentation lacking. Whether true or not, such unconfirmed anecdotes and rumours belong to the totality of Julia Pastrana's story.
21. This and the several other passages from Gunther Grass's *The Tin Drum* have been newly translated here.
22. Lerfold, unpublished manuscript.
23. Cited in Ødegaard, p. 113.
24. Jungmarker, p. 109.

Seven: Go Over Her With a Vacuum Cleaner

1. Cited in Ødegaard, p. 116.
2. Andersen and Naess.
3. Lund, interviewed by Mosander.
4. This and the other passages from Astrid Linelgren's *Emil in the Soup Tureen* have been newly translated here.
5. In the anonymous 'Reaksjon mot "Apekvinnan"'s Sverige-turné'.

6. Ibid.
7. An alternative claim has been made that the corpse on display, claimed to be that of Anna Colbjørnsen, is in fact that of another woman. See Tank, in Hals, Brænden and Johnsrud, p. 17.
8. In the anonymous 'Reaksjon mot "Apekvinnan"'s Sverige-turné'.
9. Cited in Ødegaard, p. 118.
10. Lund interviewed by Kersti Fagerheim, 26 April 1974, *VG*, cited in Ødegaard, p. 118
11. Ibid, p. 120.
12. Tore Skofterød rang us having read about Julia on the internet in spring 2001. He wanted to correct certain inaccuracies in our account. He has been of inestimable help and, in the course of several long conversations, described what happened when he and his friends found Julia. His version is taken as the correct one. We have also spoken to his childhood friend Torgeir, who supports Skofterød's version. Torgeir wants no further involve-ment in the affair, and therefore remains anonymous.
13. This, and the following two quotations, are taken from Askeland.
14. Sokolov, p. 468.
15. This and the next quotation come from Bjørnlid.
16. The record of the proceedings from which this citation was taken may be found at: www.admin.ueo.no/kollegiet/møter/kart_prot94/mote12/protokoll_12_94.html
17. In an interview with Bugge.
18. In an interview with Krohn.
19. From the anonymous article 'Julia Pastrana i boks'.

Bibliography

'A case in point' (anon.). *Appleton's Journal*, New York, 19 August 1871, vol. 6, no. 125, p. 222.

'A new process of embalming and preserving the human body' (anon.). *Lancet*, London, 15 March 1862.

Andersen, Tore and Næss, Stig, 'Apekvinnen på nattlig tur i Oslo. Julia Pastrana fram i rampelyset igjen' [Ape woman on night tour in Oslo. Julia Pastrana in the limelight again]. *VG*, Oslo, 2 June 1994.

'Apekvinnan Julia skal gravlegges' [Ape woman Julia to be buried]. *VG*, Oslo, 24 April 1997.

Aasbreen, Magne. 'Den styggaste kvinna i verda' [The ugliest woman in the world]. *Syn og Segn*, no. 1, 1999.

Askeland, Ragnar. 'Den utstoppede "apekvinnan". Kriminal Journalen fant henne igjen' [The stuffed "Ape woman". Kriminal Journalen re-discovered her]. *Kriminal Journalen*, Oslo, February 1990.

Berger, Thor Inge. 'Jeg har tørka støv av Julia' [I have dusted off Julia]. *Demokraten*, Fredrikstad, 8 May 1993.

Berthelsen, Herman. *Skjeggete damer og siamesiske tvillinger. Fra Tivoli til Big Brother*. Oslo, 2002.

Best, Geoffrey. *Mid-Victorian Britain 1851–75*. London, 1985.

Bjørnklid, Ole Martin. 'Ingen eier "apekvinnan" Julia' [No one owns the 'ape-woman' Julia]. *Aftenposten*, Oslo, 2 June 1994.

Bogdan, Robert. *Freak Show: Presenting Human Oddities for Amusement and Profit*. Chicago, 1987.

Bompas, George C. *Life of Frank Buckland*. London, no date, *c.* 1914.

Bondeson, Jan and Miles, A.E.W. 'Julia Pastrana, the non-descript: an example of congenital, generalized hypertrichosis terminalis with gingival hyperplasia'. *American Journal of Medical Genetics*, 47, 1993, pp. 198–212.

Bondeson, Jan. *A Cabinet of Medical Curiosities*. Ithaca, 1997.

———. *Medicinhistorisk kuriosakabinett*. np,1992.

———. *The Two-Headed Boy, and other Medical marvels*. New York, 2000.

Buckland, Francis T. *Curiosities of Natural History*, 2nd Series. London, 1866.

Bugge, Stella. 'Ulvekvinne skal ikke begraves' [Wolf woman shall not be buried]. *VG*, Oslo, 7 October 1996.

'Courrier de Londres' (anon). *L'Entr'acte*, 9 August 1857.

Crumrine, N. Ross and Weigand, Phil C. (eds). *Ejidos and Regions of Refuge in Northwestern Mexico*. Tucson, 1987.

Darwin, Charles. *The Variation of Animals and Plants Under Domestication*. London, 1868.

Drimmer, Frederick. *Very Special People: The Struggles, Loves and Triumphs of Human Oddities*. New York, 1973.

Felgenhauer, W.R. 'Hypertrichosis languinosa universalis'. *Journal de Génétique Humaine*, 17, 1969, pp. 593–9.

Fowler-Salamini, Heather and Vaughan, M.K. (eds). *Women of the Mexican Countryside, 1850–1990*. Tucson, 1994.

Frost, Thomas. *Circus Life and Circus Celebrities*. London, 1875.

Fuchs, J. *Über Tricosen, besonders die der Julia Pastrana*. Doctoral dissertation. Bonn, 1917.

Gould, George M. and Pyle, Walter L. *Anomalies and Curiosities of Medicine*. Philadelphia, 1901.

Hammer, Carl and Bosker, Gideon. *Freak Show: Sideshow Banner Art*. San Francisco, 1996.

Hansen, Frode. 'Striden om "apekvinnan" kan være løst' [Row over 'Ape-woman' may be resolved]. *Dagbladet*, Oslo, 24 April 1997.

Hegna, Liv. 'Ulvekvinnen Julia bør inn i nytt museum' [Wolf-woman Julia should go into new museum]. *Aftenposten*, Oslo, 29 November 1993.

Howell, Michael and Ford, Peter. *The True History of the Elephant Man*. London, 1980.

Humphries, Barry (ed). *Bizarre*. London, 1965.

Hutchinson, H.N. et al. *The Living Races of Mankind*. London, 1900.

Ilboe, Fredrik. Å, *for en tid!* Oslo, 1969.

'Julia Pastrana i boks' [Julia Pastrana in box]. *Uniform*, 19, Oslo, 1997.

Jungmarker, Gunnar. *Gycklare: Max Alexander, Brazil Jack och Showfamiljen Rhodin*. Stockholm, 1979.

Krohn, Astrid Løken. 'Bevares for vitenskapen' (Preserved for science). *Aftenposten*, Oslo, 26 January 1997.

Khromov, S.S. et al. (eds). 'On the way to bourgeois reforms' (anony-mous article). *History of Moscow: An Outline*. Moscow, 1981.

Kunhardt, Philip et al. *P.T. Barnum: America's Greatest Showman*. New York, 1995.

Lerfald, Georg. *Min minnebok*. Unpublished personal memoir, Fredrikstad, 1985.

Lerfald, Georg. *Min minnebok nr. II*. Unpublished personal memoir, Fredrikstad, 1991.

Leroi, Armand Marie. *Mutants. On Genetic Variety and the Human Body*. New York, 2003.

Lindgren, Astrid. *Emil in the Soup Tureen*. Chicago, 1963.

Lumholtz, Carl. *Unknown Mexico: A record of five years' exploration among the tribes of the Sierra Madre; in the Tierra Caliente of Tepic and Jalisco; and among the Tarascos of Michoacan*. New York, 1902.

Lyman, Elizabeth. *The Story of New York*. New York, 1964. Revd edn 1975.

Magitot, E. 'Les hommes velus.' *Gazette médicale de Paris*, series 4:2, 1873, p. 613.

Manssurow, N.P. *Klinicheskii sbornik po dermatologii sifilogii*. Moscow, 1889. no. 3.

Mannix, Daniel P. *Freaks: We Who are Not as Others*. London, 1976.

Måseide, Per Helge. 'Ønsker "Apekvinne" i graven' [Wishes 'Apewoman' buried] *Aftenposten*. Oslo, 30 November 1994.

Maxwell, Anne. *Colonial Photography and Exhibitions: Representations of the native and the making of European identities*. London, 1999.

Miles, A.E.W. 'Julia Pastrana: the bearded lady'. *Proceedings of the Royal Society of Medicine*, 67. London, 26 March 1973, pp. 160–64.

Morris, Desmond and Ramona. *Men and Apes*. New York, 1968.

Mosander, Jan. 'Apekvinnan på turné igen – 110 år efter sin död' [Apewoman on the road again – 110 years after her death]. *Expressen*, Stockholm, 2 November 1969.

Munby, Arthur. *Relicta: Verses*. London: Bertram Dobell, 1909.

Muus, Rudolf. *Gamle Kristianiaminder*. Kristiania, 1923.

Nilssen, F.H. 'Andaktsbok for Jonas Ramus' [Communion service book, Jonas Ramus's best seller]. In Fred Harald Nilssen, (ed). *Ringerike 2000*, no.72. Hønefoss, 2000.

Ødegaard, Jac. Røken. *Den Store Tivoliboka*. Oslo, 1986.

Olea, Héctor R. 'Gobernantes del estado de Sinaloa' in Ortega, Sergio and Manón, E.L. (eds), *Sinaloa, Textos de su Historia*. San Juan, 1987.

Orlean, Susan. *The Orchid Thief*. New York, 2000.

Otto, Hermann Waldemar. See Saltarino.

Parker, Mike. *The World's Most Fantastic Freaks*. London, 1983.

Purcell, Rosamund. *Special Cases: Natural Anomalies and Historical Monsters*. San Francisco, 1997.

Rasch, C. *Hudens Sygdomme og deres Behandling*. Copenhagen, 1909.

Reade, Charles. *A Terrible Temptation: A Story of the Day*. Leipzig, 1872. (First published in London, 1871.)

'Reaksjon mot "Apekvinnan's" Sverige-turné' [Reaction against Ape-woman's Swedish tour]. *Aftenposten*, Oslo, 19 March 1973.

Saltarino, Signor [Otto, Hermann Waldemar, pseud.]. *Fahrend Volk: Abnormitäten, kuriositäten und interessante Vertreter der wanderden Künstlerwelt*. Leipzig, 1895.

Sheridan, Paul. *Penny Theatres of Victorian London*. London, 1981.

Snigurowicz, Diana. 'Sex, simians and spectacle in nineteenth-century France; or how to tell a "man" from a monkey'. *Canadian Journal of History*, xxxiv:1, Saskatoon, April 1999, pp. 51–82.

Snyder, Robert W. *The Voice of the City: Vaudeville and Popular Culture in New York*. New York, 1989.

Sokolov [Sukolov], J. 'Julia Pastrana and her child'. *Lancet*, 3 May 1862, pp. 467–9.

Steck, Francis Borgia. *Motolina's History of the Indians of New Spain*. Washington, 1951.

Stenaas, Pål. 'Nytt sirkusliv for apekvinne' [New circus life for ape-woman]. *Aftenposten*, Oslo, 3 June 1964.

Strand, Tor. 'Ulvevinnen skal få hvile' [The wolf woman will rest in peace]. *Aftenposten*, Oslo, 27 November 1993.

Stølan, Jorunn. 'Ulvekvinnen på museum' [Wolf woman at museum]. *VG*, Oslo, 3 May 1994.

Svenvold, Mark. *Elmer McCurdy: The Misadventures in Life and Afterlife of an American Outlaw*. New York, 2002.

Sweet, Matthew. 'The freak show is dead. Long live the freak show!' *Independent*, London, 12 November, 1999.

Tank, Roar. 'Når Engebret Færden kom på aften-visit' [When Engebret Færden came on an evening visit]. In Ellen Hals, Ola Brænden and Hans Jonsrud, *Ringerike 1938–9*, Hønefosse, 1938.

Thompson, C.J.S. *The History and Lore of Freaks*. London, 1930.

Thomson, Rosemarie Garland (ed.). *Freakery: Cultural Spectacles of the Extraordinary Body*. New York, 1996.

Tomes, C.S. *Transactions of the Odontological Society of Great Britain*, no. 6, 1874.

Treves, Sir Frederick. *The Elephant Man and Other Reminiscences*. London, 1923.

'Un enfant velue' (anon.). *La Nature*, 12 May 1883, p. 384.

Van Hare, G. *Fifty Years of a Showman's Life, or the Life and Travels of Van Hare by himself*. London, 1888.

Waage, Gry et al. *Oslo i fest og glede*. Oslo, 1994.

Wickman, P.R. 'The most famous Indian of his day. Death of Osceola'. *The Seminole Tribune* vol. xx, no. 19, Hollywood, Florida, 23 January 1998.

Wilson, Gahan. *The Big Book of Freaks: 50 Amazing Tales of Human Oddities*. New York, 1996.

Zbarsky, Ilya and Hutchinson, Samuel. *Lenin's Embalmers*. London, 1999.

INTERNET RESOURCES

Tribble, Scott L. 'Giants in the Head: The Cardiff Giant in American Historical Consciousness 1869–1998'. At www.stribble.com/cardiffgiant/

FILMS

Browning, Todd. *Freaks*. Feature film, USA, 1932.

Ferreri, Marco. *La Donna Scimmia* (*The Ape Woman*). Feature film, Italy/France, 1963.

Maseko, Zola. *The Life and Times of Sara Bartmann*. Documentary, 1999.

Lynch, David. The Elephant Man. Feature film, UK/USA, 1980.

Index

Notes: numbers in brackets preceded by *n* are note numbers. Julia Pastrana is abbreviated to JP. Major entries are in chronological order, where appropriate.